YORKSI DAL]

CW00420625

WALKS FOR MOTORISTS

Compiled by members of
The Ramblers Association
West Riding Area

30 Walks with sketch maps

COUNTRYSIDE BOOKS
NEWBURY BERKSHIRE

*Countryside Books' walking guides cover most areas of England
and include the following series:*

*County Rambles
Walks For Motorists
Exploring Long Distance Paths
Literary Walks
Pub Walks*

A complete list is available from the publisher.

First Published by Frederick Warne Ltd

This edition published 1991
Reprinted 1993

© The Ramblers' Association
West Riding Area 1991

COUNTRYSIDE BOOKS
3 Catherine Road
Newbury
Berkshire

ISBN 1 85306 116 6

Cover photograph taken near Grassington by Andy Williams

Publishers' Note

While every care has been taken in the compilation of this book, the publishers cannot accept responsibility for any inaccuracies. But things may have changed since the book was published; paths are sometimes diverted, a concrete bridge may replace a wooden one, stiles disappear.

The length of each walk is given in miles and kilometres, but within the text imperial measurements are quoted. It is useful to bear the following approximations in mind: 5 miles = 8 kilometres, ½ mile = 805 metres, 1 metre = 39.4 inches.

Produced through MRM Associates Ltd., Reading
Printed by J. W. Arrowsmith Ltd., Bristol

Contents

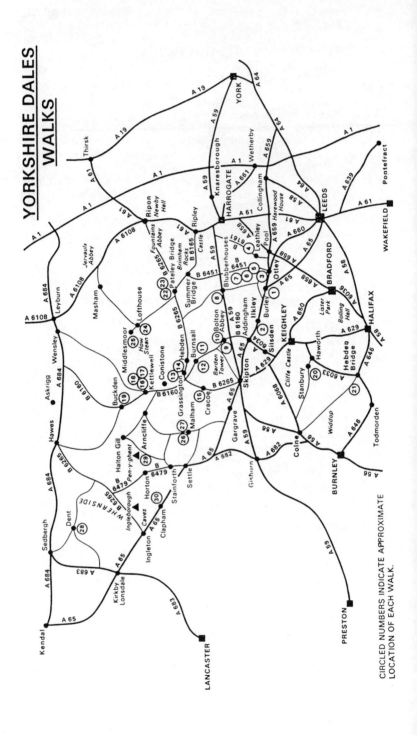

YORKSHIRE DALES
WALKS

CIRCLED NUMBERS INDICATE APPROXIMATE LOCATION OF EACH WALK.

Introduction

This book of short walks is intended to provide an introduction to some of the finest landscapes within and on the fringes of the Yorkshire Dales National Park, although as the book was first produced by ramblers from Leeds and Bradford with their fellow walkers from the West Yorkshire conurbation in mind, it concentrates on the south and south-west of the Park, and makes two excursions into the South Pennines.

All the walks are circular, and although some are moderately strenuous, all are suitable for families. All are on rights of way or permissive paths, in designated access areas or over land where access has traditionally not been disputed (but see the note to Walk 30).

As one of the first essentials of a book of rambles such as this is to give clear and unambiguous descriptions of the routes, that has been the first priority, and background information, historical, botanical, and so on, has been kept to a minimum. Further information about the area can readily be obtained from the excellent local Tourist Information Centres and National Park Information Centres (in Grassington, Malham and Clapham).

The sketch maps are intended to make it easy to find the start of the walk and to show the general pattern of the route, but should not be relied on for specific details, and they are not to scale. At the start of each walk the relevant Ordnance Survey 1:50 000 Landranger and 1:25 000 Pathfinder (or Outdoor Leisure) maps are indicated. The Landranger maps are useful for a more general orientation, but the larger scale maps are more useful to walkers.

Although none of these walks is in itself arduous, weather conditions can make the higher or more exposed routes more difficult, and walkers should pay attention to the local weather forecast and make sure that they are adequately dressed and shod. Mud is liable to be encountered almost anywhere after rain. Remember too that limestone can be slippery when wet. Keep an eye open for bulls, as the law unfortunately allows beef bulls to pasture with their herds in fields crossed by public footpaths, and give them a wide berth.

If you enjoy the walks in this book, please consider joining the Ramblers' Association, which is dedicated both at national and local levels to protecting the priceless inheritance of our public rights of way. There will be a local group near your home, and further information can be obtained from:

The Ramblers' Association,
1/5 Wandsworth Road,
London SW8 2XX.

In the 21 years since it was first published, many members of the West Riding Area of the Ramblers' Association have contributed to the successive editions of this book; particular mention must be made of Tom Wilcock and Raymond Cohen for their work in the early days, and Colin Newton and Ken Butterworth of the Lower Wharfedale Group for later revisions. The present edition has been entirely revised and the maps updated by Douglas Cossar, who would be grateful, via the publishers, for comments, suggestions and details of any problems encountered on the walks.

Finally, all responsible ramblers will want to observe the Country Code:

> Guard against all risks of fire
> Fasten all gates
> Keep dogs under proper control
> Keep to paths across farmland
> Avoid damaging fences, hedges and walls
> Leave no litter
> Safeguard water supplies
> Protect wildlife, wild plants and trees
> Go carefully on country roads
> Respect the life of the countryside

BURLEY IN WHARFEDALE AND BURLEY MOOR

WALK 1

★

4½ miles (7¼ km)

1:50 000 Sheet 104; 1:25 000 Sheet SE04/14

This walk leaves the fields and woods around Burley in Wharfedale to reach open moors with lovely views. Drive up Station Road in Burley in Wharfedale off the A65 and turn left into Grange Road. Park here. (There is alternative parking just off the A65 behind the Queen's Hall — see sketch-map.)

Return to Station Road and turn left up it. Pass under the railway bridge and take the first lane on the left (Hag Farm Road). The tarmac ends at a large house on the left (West Winds) and you reach open country. Just after a slight right-hand bend look out for a gap-stile in a recess in the fence on the right. Pass through and walk straight across the field to a step-stile beside a gate ahead.

Continue straight across the next field to a gateway, then over the slab bridge and straight ahead through the wood. On leaving the wood, walk straight across the clearing up to a step-stile to the left of a gate ahead. Now the clear path leads up between an old wall and a fence to a kissing-gate into a field. Continue uphill with the remains of a fence to your left. At the top find a stile at the left-hand end of the facing hedge, cross it and keep on up with the fence to your left to another stile, then pass to the left of a cottage and up the access drive, which bends right and then left to reach the road beside the carpark of the Hermit Inn in Burley Woodhead. The pub is named after a 19th century character, Job Senior, who lived in a hut by the Coldstone Beck on the edge of Burley Moor.

Turn left along the road past the pub (care: narrow road!) to a PF (public footpath) sign on the right halfway along Prospect Row cottages. Cross the stile and bear half-left up the slope to a gap-stile to the right of a gate. Do not go through this, but turn right and follow the wall on your left up to another stile in the field corner. Keep on up with the wall/fence to your left, through another gap-stile and up to pass to the left of the tall isolated house ahead.

Turn right up the lane. Now the views open up: Otley Chevin, Otley, Almscliffe Crag and Wharfedale. Bear left with the lane and through a

7

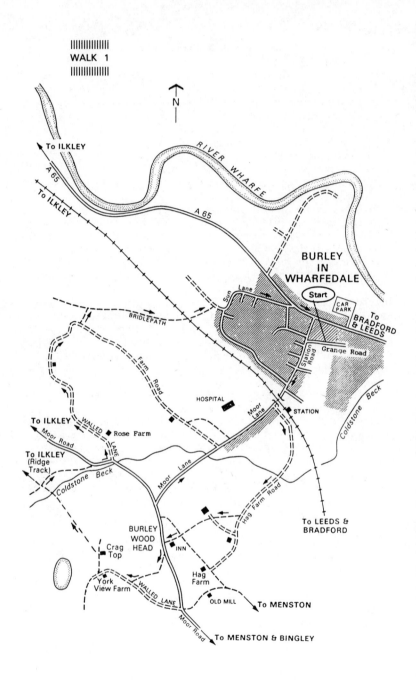

gate onto the open moor. The house on the left is York View, from where, it is said, one can see York Minster 25 miles away. Turn right and follow the wall on your right. Just before you reach two large barns on the right at the next farm find a path bearing left across the moor. In a few yards it passes above and to the left of an old quarry. Soon you are walking on a clear path through bracken. The views are magnificent, from Guiseley round to Beamsley Beacon.

Eventually the clear path leads down to cross Coldstone Beck in its ravine. Climb up the other side but, before you reach the top, bear right on a descending grassy path. When you reach a cross path turn right and descend with the beck in its deep ravine on your right to join the road on a bend. Bear right down the road, but at the end of the lay-by on the right take the path over the gorse-covered hillock. It leads back to the road: cross over and walk left for a few yards to take the stony access road to Rose Farm on the right.

At Rose Farm keep left with the track, round to the left of the buildings, and follow its winding course, at one point passing straight through another farmyard. Shortly after the second sharp right-hand bend after this farm, bear left down a fenced track over a cattle-grid. Where the track turns left, turn right through a gate, on a clear path.

When you reach a meadow, walk straight across it to the right-hand of two facing gates, then straight on parallel to the hedge on the right. The path leads down to a gate across the railway (care!). Follow the track down to a T-junction and turn right. This is Sun Lane, which you follow back to the A65. Bear right to the centre of the village and your car.

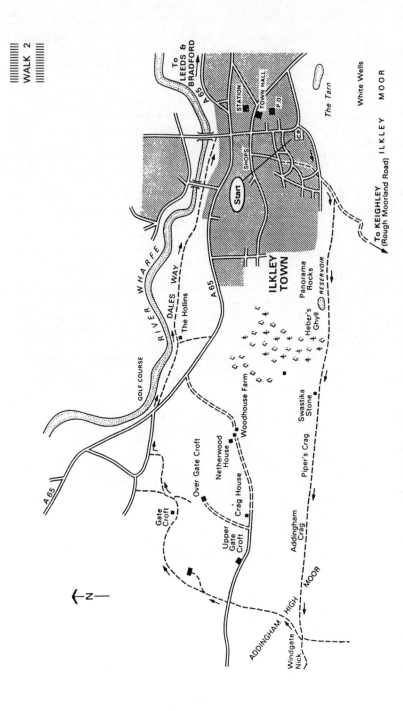

WALK 2

To LEEDS & BRADFORD

STATION

TOWN HALL

P.O

SHOPS

Start

C.P.

The Tarn

White Wells

ILKLEY MOOR

To KEIGHLEY
(Rough Moorland Road)

ILKLEY TOWN

Panorama Rocks

RESERVOIR

Heber's Ghyll

RIVER WHARFE

GOLF COURSE

DALES WAY

The Hollins

A 65

A 65

Swastika Stone

Woodhouse Farm

Netherwood House

Crag House

Over Gate Croft

Gate Croft

Upper Gate Croft

Piper's Crag

Addingham Crag

ADDINGHAM HIGH MOOR

Windgate Nick

N

ILKLEY MOOR AND WINDGATE NICK

WALK 2

★

6½ miles (10½ km)

1:50 000 Sheet 104; 1:25 000 Sheet SE04/14

Ilkley is the starting point for this walk on easy moorland and riverside paths. It follows some delightful field paths which are a pleasant exercise in route-finding and a short section of the Dales Way. There are glorious views of mid-Wharfedale.

From the traffic lights in the centre of Ilkley drive up Brook Street (signposted Ilkley Moor) and at the top bear left then immediately right up the one-way Wells Road; over the cattle grid at the top there is a carpark immediately on the right. Start here.

Leave the carpark and turn right up the road. Where the road forks go left (no through road), and 50 yards before the road crosses a bridge (by a sheep warning sign) bear right onto a grassy track, cross a footbridge and continue with a high wall and houses to the right along the edge of the moor. After the houses end you pass a reservoir, then 50 yards before a wooden footbridge over a ghyll, and a wood, find a clear path ascending half-left which leads across the ghyll by a plank bridge about 50 yards upstream from the wooden footbridge.

Pass through a gap in an old wall with the upright of an iron gate, and the railings protecting the Swastika Stone can be seen ahead; it has fine views from Otley Chevin round to Beamsley Beacon and Addingham.

Continue along the moor edge path. The following are the features you encounter en route (in order): gap-stile, wide walled lane, wall to your right, gap-stile, a few low trees, broken down wall to cross (with a gap-stile a few yards left of the crossing point), gap-stile, ladder-stile, large cairn on left, step-stile, series of cairns, step-stile, large isolated boulder, three step-stiles, cairned path through heather some yards left of the edge of the moor, and soon there is a view left to the two mushroom-like Doubler Stones and to Airedale. When you reach a crossing of paths with a gap-stile in the wall 60 yards to your left, walk forward a few yards for the view from the rock, then return and take the path descending through the cleft of Windgate Nick.

At the foot of the crag take the right fork, which leads down quite gently to a stile in the wall at the bottom. Over it, head straight down the rough pasture (towards the houses) to meet a wall coming from the left and curving downhill; keep this wall on your left and you will reach a stile in it in the bottom corner. Cross this and keep on down, now with the wall on your right, to a stile onto a minor road.

Cross straight over and go down the access road to Stegg House Farm with the beck to your right. Just before the road crosses the beck by a cattle grid bear left (PF — public footpath — sign) along with a fence to your left. In a few yards you reach a gap-stile into a field. Now the route-finding should be fun! Walk straight forward down the slope, soon to pick up a broken wall; keep to the right of it and and where it bears left bear left with it, but in a few yards bear right again, down the slope to a step-stile in the cross-wall at the bottom.

Continue down with the wall to your left to the next stile, then straight down across the next field to the next one. Now bear slightly right, to drop to a stile in the bottom right-hand corner of the field. Ignore the footbridge on the left and walk straight on over the next stile. The path climbs, keeping close to the edge of the field on the left, then at the top of the rise bears right and drops to cross another side beck.

Walk along the middle of the next long field, tending slightly to the left-hand side, to keep to the left of a beck which is marked by a line of trees, and follow the left-hand edge of the field to a gate just before the next farm. Through it, pass to the right of the barn, through another gate, and straight on along the farm access road. You cross a cattle grid and are joined by another lane from the right.

A hundred yards further on, before you reach two large old trees, bear half-right off the track and down the slope to the beck; ignore a slab bridge across it and keep on with the beck to your right, to cross it by a stony ford. Walk forward, then bear right with the fence on your right; the fence becomes a wall and turns left. Ignore the gap-stile in it, and follow it along to the farm, turning left again at the end of the field to walk along the rear of the farm and follow the fence on your right to a gate and a road. Now route-finding is easy again!

Turn right along the road. When you reach the A65 cross straight over (care!) to find a path which bears right and winds through the trees to the old road. Cross this and bear left for a few yards then sharp right (PF sign to Ilkley) with the river Wharfe to your left. (You are now on the Dales Way.) Follow the riverside track/path to get back to Ilkley.

Be careful at one point to drop down a few steps to cross a footbridge on the left. Just after passing a pumping station you cross another footbridge and go though a kissing-gate to keep alongside the fence on your right. Through another (white) kissing-gate bear left, with the fence now to your left, and through the next one again bear slightly left; through the next one bear right along the fence on your right, and through the next one slightly left; through the next one bear right along the access road to the Tennis Club.

Where the drive bears right keep straight on along the footpath to the 17th century bridge in Ilkley, the official start of the Dales Way. At the near end of the bridge a stile leads down a few steps to the continuation of the riverside path. Go up the steps to the right of the next bridge onto the road and turn right up the road. At the traffic lights either go right to visit the parish church and the Manor House Museum behind it, or cross straight over to return to the car.

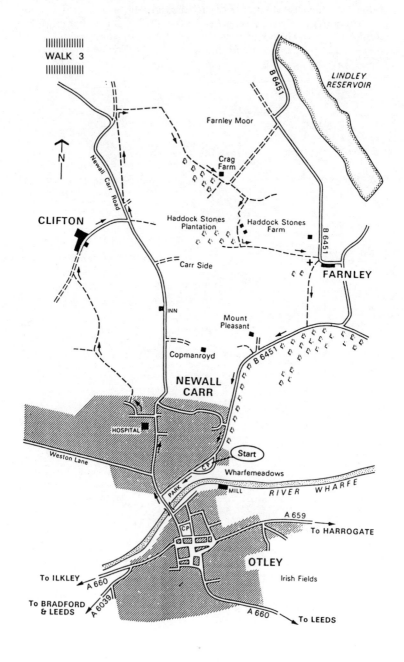

WALK 3

LINDLEY
RESERVOIR

B 6451

Farnley Moor

N

Newall Carr Road

Crag
Farm

CLIFTON

Haddock Stones
Plantation

Haddock Stones
Farm

B 6451

Carr Side

FARNLEY

INN

Mount
Pleasant

B 6451

Copmanroyd

NEWALL
CARR

HOSPITAL

Start

Weston Lane

PARK

Wharfemeadows

MILL

RIVER WHARFE

A 659

CP

To HARROGATE

OTLEY

Irish Fields

To ILKLEY

A 660

To BRADFORD
& LEEDS

A 6038

A 660

To LEEDS

CLIFTON AND FARNLEY

WALK 3

★

6 miles (9½ km)

1:50 000 Sheet 104; 1:25 000 Sheets SE04/14, 24/34

Old tracks and field paths are followed to the delightful hamlet of Clifton. From Otley town centre cross the bridge over the river Wharfe, turn first right into Farnley Lane and first right again into a No Through Road which leads to a carpark and picnic site. Park here (this area becomes very busy on summer weekends).

Go through the gateway into the park and turn right, making your way down to the riverside path, and follow it past the children's play area and paddling pool, the café and bowling-green to Otley Bridge. There go up the steps and turn right along the road, passing Farnley Lane end and continuing up the hill until you reach Wharfedale General Hospital. Just after it turn left into Carr Bank Bottom, which becomes St Richards Road, then first right into St Davids Road.

Just before the left-hand bend at the top, follow the PF (public footpath) sign (Clifton and Weston) right between houses. Cross the stile into the field and take the left fork, keeping close to the hedge on the left. Shortly you leave the hedge, only to meet up with it again in the top corner of the field. Cross the stile and walk straight up the centre of the field to another stile by a gate. The clear track continues to another stile by a gate and should be followed until you cross a stile into a lane.

Turn left along the lane, keeping right at the T-junction. Follow the lane through the delightful hamlet of Clifton with its lovely old houses, and keep on it until you reach the Otley to Blubberhouses road. Here turn left and follow the road until just after the access road to Maverick Farm on the right, where there is a PF sign and stile. Cross it and turn left to follow the fence on the left along to another stile in the far corner of the field. Cross this and turn sharp right along the edge of the field, turning left near the top along a stony track which leads past the farm buildings.

At the end of the field cross the stile and walk straight on, still with the fence to your right. At the end of this field cross the stile by the gate and bear slightly left to a step-stile in the far left-hand corner of the field. Ignore the tarmac road ahead and turn sharp right down a grassy lane. Pass through a gate and continue with the wall on your left. Through the next gateway keep forward in the old walled lane, but in 50 yards turn right with the track to follow the wall on your right. You are now walking parallel to Lindley Reservoir in the Washburn valley down on your left.

Soon you enter a wide walled lane which leads down by the side of the wood to Crag Farm. Pass to the right of the farm, through a gate and along the access road. Shortly after this turns sharp left go through the first gate on the right and walk along the top edge of the field to a gate in the far corner. Pass through and turn sharp right, following the wall on your right. At the top of the field turn left and walk along as far as the first gate in the wall on your right.

The next section of the path has been diverted. Go through the gate and bear slightly left across the field to a ladder-stile by a wooden pylon (right of the trees, left of a ramshackle shed). Over the stile walk forward a few yards to a stile onto the access road of Haddockstones Farm and then straight down the road. This soon bears left and should be followed all the way to the road just past Farnley church.

Turn right down the road to the corner, then right again though the gateway (PF sign) leading to the church, but after 15 yards pass through the small white gate on the left. Bear half-right past a solitary oak tree to a stile in the bottom right-hand corner of the field. Cross it and continue along the hedge on your right. Cross another stile and then keep straight on to pick up another hedge on your right which leads to a stile onto Farnley Lane (the Farnley Hall estate is straight ahead).

Cross the road and turn right along the pavement. When you reach Otley, look out for Athelstan Lane on the right; opposite it on the left is a paved path which leads back to the car.

THE LEATHLEY LANES

WALK 4

★

6 miles (9½ km)

1:50 000 Sheet 104; 1:25 000 Sheet SE24/34

Along old tracks and field paths this easy walk passes through pastoral scenery with fine views of Lower Wharfedale. Park your car on high ground opposite the church at Leathley (GR 232 470).

Take the road signposted Stainburn, in front of the old school and almshouses, and almost immediately fork right onto the drive to Leathley Hall. Pass to the left of the Hall and where the lane forks keep left. Pass through two gates close together into a grassy lane lined by some old trees. On reaching a fence ahead, bear left with the track to a stile and continue up the slope with the fence to your left. This is Leafield Lane.

Through another gate, go straight forward with a fence now on your right to pass between old hawthorn trees and through two gates close together with a farm down to your right. Continue along the lane to within a field-length of a wood, cross a stile by a gate and bear half-left across the field to the far corner of Riffa Wood, where you ford a beck and cross a stile into the wood.

Walk up the clear path, the age of which is shown by the remains of causey stones, passing a rock curiously carved as a head on the left. Enter a field at the top of the wood and immediately turn left to a gate at the corner of the wood. Go through and across the field, bearing slightly left to a large gate.

Through the gate you follow the fence on your right, ignoring gates in it, and soon picking up a clear track which you follow all the way to the road in Stainburn; on the way you will bear slightly left to cross a beck and then closely follow the left-hand edge of the fields, interrupted by a short stretch of walled lane.

Turn left along the road and at the second bend you will find a kissing-gate on the right; pass through and follow the wall/fence on your right up to another kissing-gate into the churchyard of Stainburn church. Of Norman origin, it has an 800-year-old font and lovely views from its porch to greet you as you emerge.

On leaving the porch turn right and follow the path to the road. Turn right along it and walk through Braythorn as far as Gale Lane, a narrow

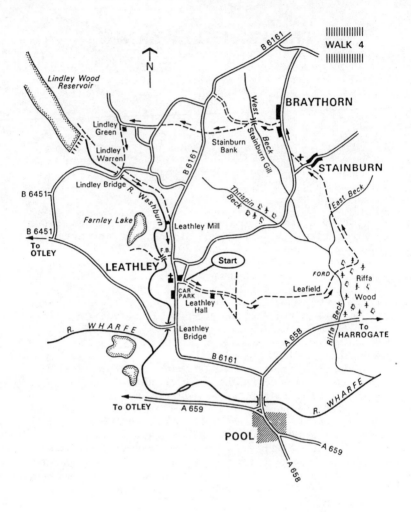

grassy track on the left immediately before the former Methodist Chapel. The lane descends to cross West Beck by Green Bridge. Just after the bridge cross the stile on the left and follow the clear path up the right-hand edge of the field, soon leaving it to bear left up to wooden stiles halfway along a double wooden fence at the top. Cross them and make for another stile to the left of a short stretch of wall ahead. Climb this and follow the left side of the hedge to a stone stile and cross the next field to a step-stile to the right of the farmhouse and to the left of the barns.

Pass the back door of the farm and follow the farm road to the Leathley-Killinghall road. Cross straight over this, through the large gate opposite, and bear very slightly right across the enormous field (at the time of writing the path passes to the right of a solitary tree, but as this is dead it may not last much longer) to a high step-stile on the far side. Care is needed on this very high wall. The right of way now bears half-right to the wall on the far side of the next field and then turns left along it, but you may find on the ground a clear path going straight ahead across the field instead to where the trees and the wall meet. Bear left along the fence to reach the road.

Cross it and follow the narrow road ahead to Lindley Green, ignoring a road on the left to Farnley on the way. Just after the first complex of buildings on the left, where there is a post-box and the road bends right, pass through a gate ahead and turn immediately left down the end of the building to a stile, and continue down to a wide gate in the wall ahead. Now make your way down through Lindley Warren, keeping about 20 yards away from the wall on your left. The path is clear all the way down to a stile, then follows the wallside down to a gap-stile where you bear left to the road.

Turn right down the road to Lindley Bridge and the River Washburn. Just before the bridge pass through a stile on the left and drop down some steps to a path along a narrow goit (millrace). Follow this goit by the side of a trout farm and with the river well to your right, to a stone overflow near some cottages high up on the left. Drop right here, then bear left to a stile near the river. The path now leads between the goit and the river to Leathley Mill. When you reach the buildings cross the stile and turn left over the goit to follow the path round to the mill yard and out onto the road.

Turn right along the road, using the verge where possible, to return to the car.

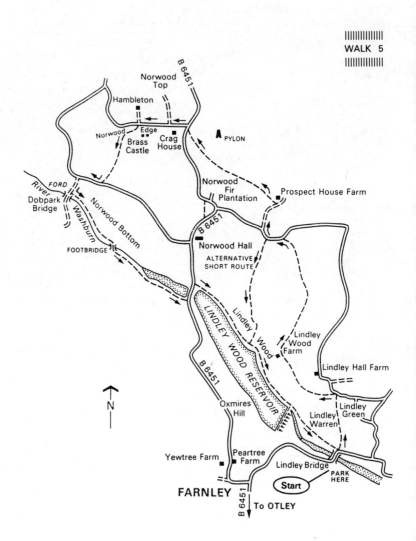

||||||||||||
WALK 5
||||||||||||

NORWOOD AND LINDLEY WOOD

WALK 5

★

7½ miles (12 km) or 4 miles (7 km)

1:50 000 Sheet 104; 1:25 000 Sheets SE05/15, 24/34, 25/35

This walk, with some fine views, follows old tracks and field paths by the riverside and through woodland. There is a shorter, alternative route. Park at Lindley Bridge (GR 224 483), which is reached by taking the B6451 Pateley Bridge road out of Otley, following it as it turns sharp left at Farnley Hall Home Farm and then taking the first fork right after this.

Cross the bridge and follow the road uphill; pass the lodge and entrance gates to Lindley Wood Reservoir on the left and bear right with the road, but in a few yards take a short track slanting back left to a gate. To the right of the gate is a gap-stile; pass through and follow the clear path up by the wall on the right (PF — public footpath — sign). Cross a stile and continue uphill with the wall, bearing slightly left at the wooden telegraph pole to cut the corner. The clear path is never far from the wall on the right and leads to a gate in the facing wall at the top. Walk up to the left of the buildings to a stile in the fence ahead and forward to the stony track on which you turn left with a wall to your right.

Emerging from the wood, cross the cattle grid and walk forward on the track to the house ahead, bearing right before the next cattle grid at the entrance to the garden and following the fence on your left along to rejoin the track which emerges from a gate on your left just over the brow of the hill. The track then swings right to contour parallel to a wood down on the left. There is a broken wall to your left. Soon you enter a walled lane. On leaving it the track descends gently towards trees.

Go through a gate and cross the beck, and continue up in the old walled lane, passing to the left of the ruined farm. The broken wall on your left leads you to another beck to be crossed, then walk forward up the facing slope with a gulley to your right. Bear left at the top of the slope to a step-stile to the right of a gate. Cross and walk forward a few yards to another stile, continuing then with the wall to your left. At the end of the field ignore the gate in the corner, cross the broken wall to the right of it and then the wooden stile three yards further on. Follow the fence/wall on your left. The wall bears left, and where it ends bear right down to the beck and walk along with the wall on your left to the road (PF sign). Turn left through the gate and along the road.

The **shorter, alternative walk** takes the next farm access road on the left (to Wood Top Farm) (PF sign) (see page 23).

For the **main walk** continue to where the road turns sharply left; here keep straight ahead (PF sign) up the access road to Prospect House Farm. Bear right at the top over the cattle grid, then turn left to pass to the left of the farm buildings; at the top of the field bear left along the concrete track to a gate. Pass through and continue with the wall to your left.

Drop to a gate in the bottom left-hand corner, pass through and walk straight across the next field to a wall, there bearing left along with this wall to your right. Where the wall turns right, bear very slightly left to a gate into the wood. Bear right immediately on the ascending path through the trees; at the top of the slope the path enters a grassy ride. You are joined by a clearer track from the right. Soon the surface deteriorates, but keep on, to reach a road through a gate.

Turn right along the road for a few yards, then left down the first minor road as far as the beginning of a wood on the left. The next section needs careful route finding. A wall runs steeply down the left side of the wood; go down for 40 yards between this wall and the wood, then follow the path as it turns right through the trees. After 40 yards turn left again, going downhill on the clear path, to pick up a wall which you follow on down, keeping it to your left. Where this wall turns right pass through a gap in it and turn right along a clear cross-track.

A hundred yards further on turn sharp left down a track, in fact down the extremely stony ribbon of a collapsed wall. When you meet a facing wall go right along it for a yard or two to a corner, then keep on down with the wall to your left to cross a collapsed stile in the next facing wall and continue along the edge of two fields with the wall to your left to a gate and the road. Now the route finding is easy again!

Turn right along the road. Where it forks keep left, and a few yards further on turn sharp left down a road (Unsuitable for Motors) towards Dobpark Bridge. When you reach the river Washburn go over the stile on your left (although a detour right for a few yards to admire this fine old bridge is recommended) and walk forward to join the clear track. Cross a stile by a gate and keep straight ahead on the track. Soon the track bears right to cross the river by a bridge, then bears left again.

When you reach the road turn left over the bridge, then turning right at the first opportunity through the gateway and along the track by Lindley Wood Reservoir. Follow this all the way to the next road, where you turn right for the car.

The shorter alternative: Follow the access road to Wood Top Farm, passing to the right of the buildings, until you are faced by a gate straight ahead. Go through, and straight through the long narrow field to a gate at the far end. Pass through this and continue with the wall on your left to another gate, then on with the fence on your right to another gate, and on with the wall/fence to your right to a gateway and then another gate, and on with the wall to your right, through another gate, then on with the wall to your left (there is a barn to your left). Where the wall goes left, follow it (passing through a gate); it leads to a stile into the wood, and a clear path leads down through the wood. At the track at the bottom by the reservoir, turn left, and at the next road turn right to return to the car.

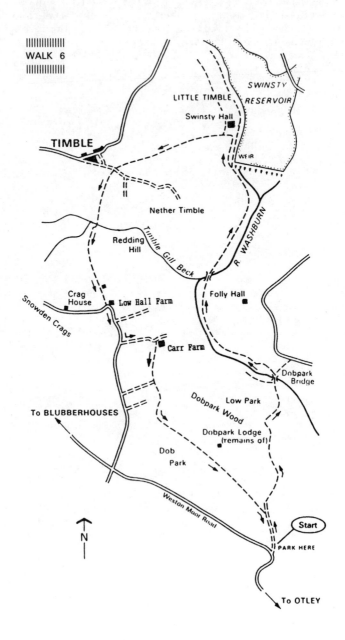

WALK 6

SWINSTY RESERVOIR

LITTLE TIMBLE

Swinsty Hall

TIMBLE

WEIR

Nether Timble

Redding Hill

Timble Gill Beck

R. WASHBURN

Folly Hall

Crag House

Snowden Crags

Low Hall Farm

Carr Farm

Dobpark Bridge

Low Park

Dobpark Wood

To BLUBBERHOUSES

Dobpark Lodge (remains of)

Dob Park

Weston Moor Road

Start

PARK HERE

N

To OTLEY

THE WASHBURN AND TIMBLE

★

7 miles (11 km)

1:50 000 Sheet 104; 1:25 000 Sheets SE05/15, 04/14

The river Washburn is never far away on this walk to Swinsty reservoir and the village of Timble. There are some glorious views from the old tracks and field paths.

From Otley take the road going north towards Blubberhouses. Shortly after passing a TV mast on the right the road makes a sharp right-hand bend closely followed by a sharp left-hand one; on this bend a no through road signposted to Dob Park forks right. Park in the layby on the right at the start of this minor road.

Follow this narrow metalled road down to the river Washburn, ignoring forks left and right. Halfway down, just past Middle Farm on the left, the lane becomes a stony track. At the river you reach Dobpark Bridge with an ancient ford beside it. The name Dobpark is derived from Dog Park and reminds us that this area was once part of the hunting-ground of the Forest of Knaresborough.

Cross the bridge and immediately go over the stile on the left, to follow the track parallel to the river as far as the next bridge back over the river. Cross this and then continue on the track as it climbs to the left-hand end of the dam of Swinsty Reservoir.

Immediately before the double gates, take the narrow path on the left which climbs steeply back up the hillside to a step-stile in the facing wall at the top. Cross this and turn right to another stile into the wood. Follow the wall on the right along, soon bearing very slightly left to keep between the left-hand pair of three parallel walls. Keep in this old walled lane until the wall on the left bears left. Bear left with it, but when you see a large old stone barn ahead, bear right to pass along the right-hand side of the barn to join a track coming from Swinsty Hall on the right. (It's worth making a detour to have a closer look at this fine old hall.)

Turn left past the end of the barn, but soon bear slightly right along a track with a wall to the left. At the top of the wood pass through a gate, cross an old lane, pass through an old gateway and walk straight up the field to a stile by a gate. Continue parallel to the wall on your right to the next stile by a gate, then keep forward, bearing very slightly left, to another stile by the next gate ahead. Follow the wall on your left — Timble village is visible ahead — to the next gate ahead, where you enter a walled lane which brings you to Timble. An old lane after the fourth building on the right (Moorview) leads to the Timble Inn, a popular source of refreshment.

From the Inn retrace your steps to the last building in Timble (the first we passed coming in) and take the first turn on the right after it down an overgrown but delightful narrow walled lane. In the bottom cross Timble Gill Beck and climb the clear path opposite. In a few yards you cross another beck, bear left alongside it (over a fence) and soon re-cross it onto a paved path with a wall to your left. Soon the path goes through a gate and now an old wall is on your right. At the end of the field a gate on the right leads into a walled lane, which soon turns sharp left and ends at a field. Follow the wall on the left to a gate and pass into an old green lane which leads to a narrow metalled road near Low Hall Farm.

Turn left along the road past the farm, then take the second farm access road on the left, which leads over a cattle-grid. At Carr Farm the footpath has been diverted. Turn right immediately before the farm (there is a ladder-stile on the left) and follow the wall on your left along to another ladder-stile in the corner of the field. Cross it and turn left down the edge of the field, then right along the bottom edge to a step-stile in the next corner. Walk straight across the next field, following the line of the telephone cable, to cross an old walled lane to a gate ahead, which leads into a wide walled lane.

Cross Snowden Beck and fork right, following the lane up to the farm buildings. Walk straight through the yard to the gate opposite, ignoring the road on the right, and climb the hill ahead with the wall to your left. At the end of the field turn left through a stile in the corner and follow the fence on your right to another stile. Walk straight across the next large field, keeping about 20 yards to the right of the wood ahead, pass to the right of a jumble of stones and gorse bushes and make for the gate in the wall ahead.

This leads into a wide walled lane. The ruins of Dobpark Lodge are a field away on the left. The lane leads to Dobpark House. Forty yards before this cross the stile on your right and bear half-left round the outside of the garden fence to a stile, then half-left again across the corner of the field to another stile, then right along the access road. At the next T-junction bear right to return to the car.

SWINSTY AND FEWSTON

WALK 7

★

6 miles (10½ km)

1:50 000 Sheet 104; 1:25 000 Sheets SE05/15, 25/35

This easy walk on tracks and field paths includes almost a complete circuit of Swinsty Reservoir. There are some fine views from Swordpoint Hill.

Park in Yorkshire Water's Swinsty carpark (GR 186 537), which is reached by taking the Blubberhouses road north from Otley, turning off right on the road to Timble then keeping left at the next junction, to reach the carpark on the right, or by following the signs for Fewston from the A59 Harrogate to Skipton road or the B6451 Otley to Pateley Bridge road and crossing the Fewston Reservoir embankment to reach the carpark on the left. The carpark has toilets.

Leave the carpark and turn right into a stony lane marked 'Private Road: Authorised Vehicles Only'. Follow the reservoir on your left as far as the embankment and turn left across this. At the far side go through the gate on the right before the house (PF — public footpath — sign) and bear left to the level shelf ahead, walking across it keeping the trees to your left. The grassy path bears slightly right and drops, and at the wall corner on the left bear slightly left on a clear path to a stile in the wall ahead.

Continue forward on the clear path with the river Washburn to your right. When you come to what looks like a padlocked and barbed wired gate, there is a stile just to the left of it. Follow the riverside path to the next river bridge and there bear left with the clear track. In a few more yards, just after some water mains, bear left up a track through the trees. Follow the track up to Folly Hall, the building which soon appears ahead, ignoring a left fork into the woodland.

Pass through a gate into the farm and keep straight forward following the wall on your left to turn left before the farmhouse up the track to another gate out of the farmyard. Follow the access road to the top of the slope, there turning left (PF sign) up a walled lane, which soon bears right up to a road.

Turn left up the road. In 40 yards go through a gap-stile beside a gate in the wall on the right and follow the wall on your right. Towards the top you bear slightly left, eventually to follow a wall on your left up to a stile by a gate in the facing wall. Cross it and continue with the wall on your right. Cross the next stile in the top corner and keep on with the wall on the right to the next road.

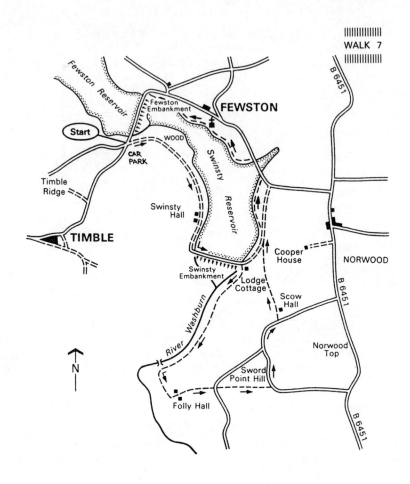

Turn left down the road and enjoy the view: the 'golf balls' of Menwith Hill Camp, and Swinsty and Fewston reservoirs are prominent. When the road forks keep right, and continue on it until you turn left into the access road to Scow Hall Farm. Walk straight through the farmyard and through the gate at the far side. The track bears left up to two facing gates; go through the left-hand, red gate. Route finding now needs a little care.

Walk forward on the track following the wall on your right down, soon leaving the track to keep with the wall, and go through a stile by a red gate on the right into a walled lane. It soon bears left. When it opens out into a small wood follow the fence on the left, but when this turns left to meet the wall keep straight ahead to pass through a red gate in the facing wall.

The walled lane leads you to the reservoir access road. Here turn left through the gate, then immediately right on the permissive path through the wood. Emerging from the wood keep forward along the clear grassy path to a large gate ahead and turn left over the embankment.

At the far side turn left through the gate and walk forward under the trees with the reservoir to your left. Follow this permissive path along the bank of the reservoir. Eventually the path rises to a small gate and the road. Turn left across the Fewston Reservoir embankment and continue up the road to return to the car.

BLUBBERHOUSES AND BRANDRITH

WALK 8

★

5 miles (8 km)

1:50 000 Sheet 104; 1:25 000 Sheet SE05/15

Starting at Blubberhouses, following old tracks and field paths through woodland and rough pasture, this walk passes close to Brandrith Crags. Blubberhouses church stands where the unclassified road from Otley meets the A59 Skipton to Harrogate road (GR 167 553); adjacent to this junction a stretch of old road forms a longish layby. Park here.

Cross the main road and walk along the grass verge in the Harrogate direction, crossing the river Washburn. Take the first turning left, signposted Pateley Bridge, and follow this minor road up Hardisty Hill as far as the entrance to Skaife Hall Farm on the left (PF — public footpath — sign to Cockbur Bank).

Follow this access road to the farm, pass to the right of the buildings and keep ahead on the track, crossing a stile by a gate with a wood on the left, then walking straight across the next field to another stile by a gate leading into a wood. The track now drops gently to cross an old mill goit (millrace).

Here bear right off the track and follow the good and level path alongside the goit, with the river down to your left, until the goit disappears into a tunnel. Now keep straight ahead to join the riverside path and follow this to the next footbridge on the left. The dam of Thruscross Reservoir looms in the distance.

Over the bridge bear right, pass through the gate and follow the track up to a crossing track. On your left at this point is a stile by a gate; cross this and walk forward to the narrow tarmaced road. Turn right along this for a yard or two to find a step-stile on the left (PF sign to Greenhow Hill Road). (The road climbs gently to the reservoir embankment, and is a pleasant detour.) The path goes straight uphill through the trees, through a gap-stile, then bears half-right up the hillside, kinking left, right and left again to cross a side-beck, then continuing up to cross a step-stile onto a tarmaced road 100 yards left of a barn.

Walk left for a few yards to find a step-stile in the fence on the right. Over this pass through two fields with the wall to your right to another step-stile in front of a barn to the right of the farm buildings. Bear slightly right into a walled lane. Brandrith Crags are visible on the moor over to your left. Where the lane ends keep straight forward through an old gateway and on with the wall on your left, but soon the clear path bears right away from the wall to the top right-hand corner of this field.

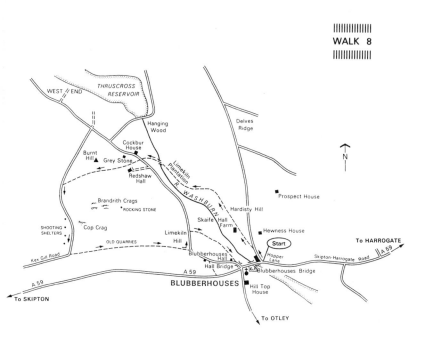

Go through the gate, walk forward for a few yards with the wall on your right, through an old gateway, then turn left to follow the wall on your left. Again the path is clear on the ground. At the end of the field go through another old gateway and continue forward now with the wall to your right. Follow this wall to a metalled road (PF sign) and turn left along it.

Where the road makes a sharp turn right, make a sharp turn left onto a track. There is a fine view to Blubberhouses church and Fewston Reservoir behind it. In a few yards do not turn right with the track but keep straight ahead over the stile by the gate onto a green track with a wall to your right. Follow this track straight on until you reach the next tarmaced road.

Here you could turn right and walk down the road to your car, but it is more pleasant to turn left and follow the road as far as the third gate on the right where there is a PF sign. Walk down the edge of the field with the wall to your right. At the bottom turn right into a walled lane and follow this lane/track all the way to a farm. Pass through the gate into the yard and bear right between the buildings to the road. Turn left down the road to your car.

31

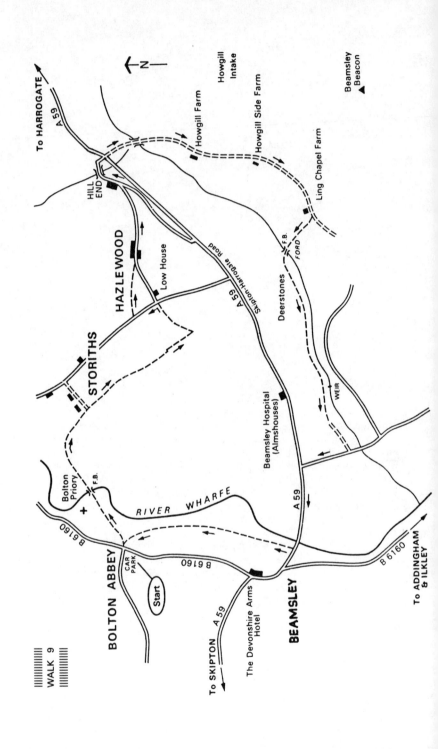

WALK 9

BOLTON ABBEY AND HAZLEWOOD

WALK 9

★

5 miles (8 km)

1:50 000 Sheet 104; 1:25 000 Outdoor Leisure Map 10 Yorkshire Dales
Southern Area

The famous Dales beauty spot of Bolton Abbey is the starting point for
this easy walk on tracks and field paths, with attractive views. Park in the
carpark at Bolton Abbey on the B6160 Ilkley–Grassington road (GR 071
538) (fee).

Return to the B6160 and enter the abbey grounds through the hole in
the wall: a clear path leads down to the abbey buildings. Bolton Priory (it
was never an abbey) was founded in 1151 and suppressed in 1539. The
nave survived, being used as the parish church; the other buildings
decayed (the gatehouse being incorporated into the Duke of
Devonshire's shooting lodge, Bolton Hall); the fine house to the south of
the priory, known as the Rectory, was built as a school and may
incorporate part of the priory infirmary; the whole is now one of the
most picturesque (and popular) sites in the Dales.

Having inspected the priory, cross the Wharfe by the footbridge and
bear left, soon forking right up some steps onto a rising path. Shortly
after passing a bench turn sharp right on the clear ascending path
signposted to Storiths. At the top there is a fine prospect of the priory.
Turn left through the gate into a walled lane and follow it to its end.
Continue up the concrete track, bearing right, left and right again
between the buildings of Storiths. Where the now tarmaced lane turns
left again, with an access road on the right, cross the step-stile in the wall
ahead (signpost) and bear half-right over the corner of the field to a
gate.

Through it, turn left and follow the wall on your left (Beamsley
Beacon can be seen on the skyline ahead) to the stile ahead, then
continue with the wall still to your left, all the way along this large field,
to a stile in the far left-hand corner. Over this bear half-right to a
ladder-stile behind a large oak tree. Walk straight over the next field to a
signpost at the wall corner ahead and follow the wall on your right along
to climb a gate in the field corner (padlocked at the time of writing).
Continue with the wall to your right over a step-stile in the next field
corner and along the edge of the next field to another step-stile ahead.

Immediately beyond this a signpost indicates a crossing of footpaths: turn left (direction: Hazlewood) and follow the wall on your left up to a gate halfway up the field. Through this the right of way bears half-right up to a gap-stile in the wall at the top, 15 yards to the right of a gate, but most walkers seem to follow the wall on the right round the edge of the field to this stile. Cross it and turn left along to the field corner, then right, with a fence to your left, to reach a minor road through a gated stile at Low House Farm.

Turn left along the road for 150 yards to a step-stile in the wall on the right (signposted Hazlewood). Bear very slightly right down the field to another step-stile in the wall at the bottom. The path is now clear as it ascends half-right, levelling out near the top to follow the fence on the left along to a gate in the corner. Through this follow the wall on your right up to the gateway ahead and bear right into the walled lane to Hazlewood.

When you reach the buildings, pass through the gate and walk forward with a shed on your right until you are forced by the house ahead to turn right through another gate, immediately followed by yet another one, after which you bear left along the front of the farmhouse and reach a minor road. Turn left along this. At a T-junction with what used to be the A59 turn left and follow this now minor road to its junction with the new A59.

Cross the main road to the PF (public footpath) signpost opposite (Howber Hill) and bear right through the gate and down the tarmaced track; soon you are in a walled lane. At the foot go through the gate and cross Kex Beck by the footbridge. Bear right alongside the beck, soon bearing slightly left to join a track to the left of a wall. Follow this wall to Howgill Farm, where you join a better track, and follow this past Howgill Side Farm and Ling Chapel Farm.

At the end of this last farm go through the gate and turn right, down by the garden wall, to cross the access road and walk forward to the first gate on the right (PF sign Deerstones). Walk straight down the rough pasture (this old county road is not marked on the 2½″ map), aiming for the right-hand of the houses ahead, to pass through a gate and follow the clear path which winds down to re-cross Kex Beck by a footbridge.

Climb the clear path to the hamlet of Deerstones, but immediately before the first house bear left through the large gate and follow the wall on your right round to a stile. With the wall still nearby on your right you soon drop to a stile close to the beck. Cross it and walk along the left-hand edge of the next field. Cross a step-stile in the wall ahead and continue with the beck on your left. Ignore a rising path forking right and keep on by the beck, soon with a wall on your right, to a step-stile in this wall at the point where there are the remains of a weir in the beck and barns on the right.

Over the stile walk straight across the middle of the next field, the reasonably clear path soon bearing slightly left and keeping along the middle of the field, rising at the far end to a step-stile. There is a caravan site over the beck on your left. When faced by a gate marked 'Private', bear right over the footbridge and cross the stile into a walled lane. Follow this down to the road at Beamsley and turn right along the road. At the A59 turn left along the footway, soon crossing to the footway on the other side.

Cross the Wharfe at Bolton Bridge and in a few yards cross the stile in the fence on the right (signposted Bolton Priory). The footpath, which is not clear on the ground, leads straight across this very large pasture, heading directly for the priory ruins which soon appear ahead, but you may prefer to follow the fence on the right which keeps closer to the river. The path becomes clearer when you pass between a steep bank on the left and the river on the right. When the field widens again bear slightly left to join the clear path up to the hole in the wall and the carpark.

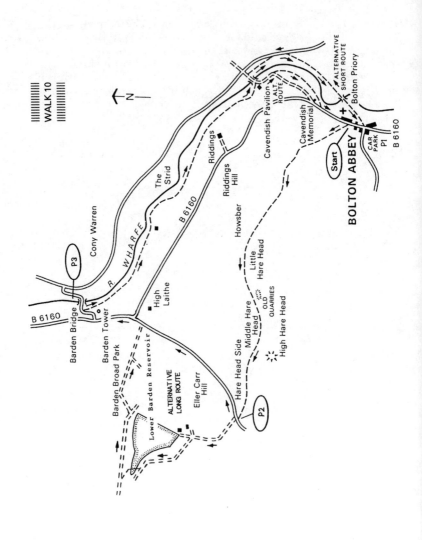

WALK 10

N

WHARFE
R.

Barden Bridge
B 6160
Cony Warren
P3
Barden Tower
Barden Broad Park
Barden Broad Park
Lower Barden Reservoir
ALTERNATIVE LONG ROUTE
Eller Carr Hill
Hare Head Side
P2
High Hare Head
OLD QUARRIES
Middle Hare Head
Little Hare Head
Howsber
High Laithe
The Strid
B 6160
Riddings
Riddings Hill
Cavendish Pavilion
ALT. ROUTE
Cavendish Memorial
Start
ALTERNATIVE SHORT ROUTE
Bolton Priory
BOLTON ABBEY
CAR PARK
P1
B 6160

BOLTON ABBEY, HARE HEAD, BARDEN TOWER AND THE STRID

WALK 10

★

8½ miles (13½ km) with a longer alternative of 9½ miles (15½ km) and a shorter one of 4½ miles (7 km)

1:50 000 Sheet 104; 1:25 000 Outdoor Leisure 10 Yorkshire Dales Southern Area

This is one of the most famous beauty spots in the Dales and the walk includes one of the loveliest stretches of the river Wharfe and some spectacular panoramic views. The walking is easy. The longer alternative lies within the Barden Moor Access Area, which may be closed on certain days in the grouse-shooting season (mid-August to December), so check in advance with the National Park office in Grassington (tel: 0756-752774).

Park in the Bolton Abbey carpark (fee) (GR 071 538) (P1 on map); alternative starts (free parking) at Hare Head Side (P2 on map GR 037 555) and Barden Bridge (P3 on map GR 053 574).

From the carpark (**P1**) return to the B6160 and turn left along it, passing under the arch of an aqueduct over the road. Go through the first large gate on the left after this (signposted to Halton Height and Rylstone), opposite Bolton Hall, the former priory gatehouse and now the Duke of Devonshire's shooting lodge, on an ascending track.

Where the track bears left to some buildings keep straight ahead through the left-hand of two facing gates (BW — bridleway — sign). Walk straight ahead, i.e. bearing left off the track, up to the right-hand end of a fenced area ahead, which is in fact a large pond (BW sign), and keep forward with the pond to your left. When the fence turns sharp left keep straight forward, soon following a wall on your left down to a large gate in the facing wall. Through this, bear right to a large gate into the wood.

Walk forward on the clear, ascending path, soon following it sharp left (BW sign); at a T-junction go right on the clear track (BW sign), soon to bear sharp left and emerge from the wood through a gate (BW sign).

You enter a very large pasture. Keep straight forward, heading for the left-hand of the three low hills on the skyline, and you will soon see that you are heading for a wall coming up from the right. There are panoramic views behind you. Pass through the gate in the wall and bear slightly left (BW sign) straight over the top of the low bump ahead. The path should be visible on the ground. The view back extends from the twin masts on Ilkley Moor round past Beamsley Beacon with its twin cairns, all the way to Barden Fell.

Cross a stony track. You meet this track again at some concrete Water Board installations. Cross it again diagonally and walk forward to a bridlegate in the wall ahead, i.e. to the left of the gate that the track passes through. The views up Wharfedale to Great Whernside and Buckden Pike and straight ahead over the Barden Moor Access Area are spectacular.

Go through the gate and bear left with the wall to your left. Soon the ruin of Barden Tower is visible down on the right. The wall leads you round to pass between the two bumps of Little Hare Head on the left and the higher Middle Hare Head on the right. When you reach the col another view opens up from Ilkley on the far left round towards Skipton and Pendle Hill in Lancashire in the distance.

Soon the path bears slightly right to climb between the two bumps of Middle Hare Head on the right and High Hare Head on the left. When you reach the col keep straight forward to a gate in the wall ahead. Lower Barden Reservoir appears ahead. The clear green way now bears left and leads to the road at Hare Head Side (**P2**).

The **main walk** turns right down the road towards Barden Bridge. Turn to [*] below.

For the **longer alternative** leave the cattle grid to your left, cross the road and climb the stile to the left of the gate opposite. Walk down the tarmaced road.

When you reach a crossroads turn left on the stony track (signposted to Upper Barden Reservoir), keep left at the next fork (there is no public access down to the right). Just before a bridge over a beck you will see a sign saying 'Danger No Public Access': this does NOT refer to the track you are on. When the reservoir narrows the track descends very gently, and just before it crosses another beck by a bridge there is a signpost pointing to Upper Barden Reservoir down a narrow path on the right, which leads in a few yards across a footbridge and a short embankment (a sign saying 'No Public Access across Embankment' does NOT refer to the short embankment straight ahead of you). The path then bears left and climbs through the bracken to join another stony track just before a cattle grid (signpost).

Turn right down the track. The reservoir is to your right. Having left the reservoir behind, you reach a fork in the track; keep left. At a T-junction keep left with the main track. You reach the road at a gate and here rejoin the route of the main walk. Turn left down to the main road and left along it.

[*] Just past the late 15th century Barden Tower fork right (the road is signposted Appletreewick and Pateley Bridge). Descend the road to the 17th century Barden Bridge (**P3**), but just before it go through the stile in the wall on the right and follow the clear track.

After passing under the arch of the next bridge over the river (it is in fact an aqueduct) and crossing the following meadow you enter Strid Wood by a stile and a footbridge. Keep left by the river. A short distance later ignore another path forking right, and now your path climbs slightly. The next fork occurs in a glade with a yellow marker post, two paths almost equal in quality, either will do, the left-hand one being slightly more adventurous.

Assuming you keep right, continue to the next fork (another yellow marker to the right, a violet marker to the left) where I would suggest you keep left and descend by a few steps. This path leads directly to the Strid [**], a wide area of rock where the Wharfe races through a deep and narrow channel. Take great care, as the rocks are often wet and slippery.

Beyond the Strid continue on the clear riverside track, and where there are forks left or right keep always on the main track, to emerge from the woods at the Cavendish Pavilion (toilets, excellent refreshments).

Cross the Wharfe by the wooden bridge and turn right through the stile (signposted Bolton Priory). Follow the path to the next stile, where turn left to the road, then right to cross a beck either by the ford or the footbridge some yards to the left. Ignore the first path on the right after the beck, but take the second (signpost). The clear path climbs quite high and gives you a superb view of the priory, before descending again to cross the river by the footbridge. On the descent you can see, to the left of the priory on the far side of the river, the clear path winding its way up to the hole in the wall which is your way back to the car after you have visited the priory itself (see notes at start of Walk 9). Emerging from the hole in the wall, cross the road half-left and take the minor road opposite back to the carpark.

Short alternative: From the Bolton Abbey carpark return to the B6160 and go through the hole in the wall giving access to Bolton Priory. Follow the clear path down to cross the Wharfe by the footbridge and keep on the clear path as it ascends the other side. Follow it all the way to a road (it climbs quite high and gives fine views back to the priory) and turn left to cross a beck by the ford or the footbridge a few yards to the right. Leave the road by the path on the left, which leads to a stile on the right and a riverside path to the wooden bridge.

Cross this and turn right into Strid Wood. Follow the main track, ignoring minor forks left and right, to the Strid (see [**] above). Return to the Cavendish Pavilion and continue through the gate by the cattle grid to the left of Wooden Bridge Lodge, then fork left and keep on the tarmac road as close to the river as you can to its end at a turning circle.

Keep straight on along the footpath, crossing the field on a clear path which climbs by steps into the trees ahead. Follow the path alongside the road to the entrance on the left into the priory grounds. After visiting the priory continue forward past the west end of the church to rejoin the path leading up to the hole in the wall and the carpark.

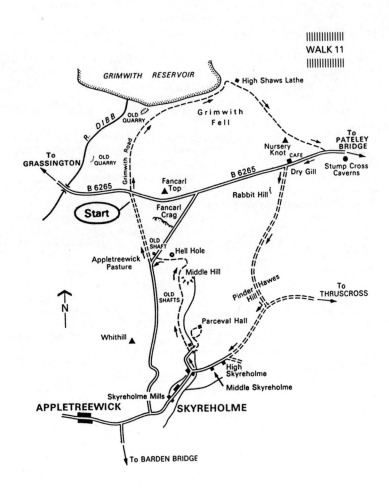

GRIMWITH RESERVOIR

High Shaws Lathe

R. DIBB

OLD QUARRY

Grimwith Fell

To PATELEY BRIDGE

Nursery Knot

OLD QUARRY

CAFE

Stump Cross Caverns

To GRASSINGTON

Grimwith Road

B 6265

Fancarl Top

B 6265

Dry Gill

Rabbit Hill

Start

Fancarl Crag

OLD SHAFT

Hell Hole

Appletreewick Pasture

Middle Hill

OLD SHAFTS

Pinder Hawes Hill

To THRUSCROSS

N

Parceval Hall

Whithill

High Skyreholme

Middle Skyreholme

Skyreholme Mills

APPLETREEWICK

SKYREHOLME

To BARDEN BRIDGE

SKYREHOLME AND GRIMWITH RESERVOIR

WALK 11

★

7 miles (11 km)

1:50 000 Sheet 99; 1:25 000 Outdoor Leisure Map 10 Yorkshire Dales Southern Area

An interesting mixture of gritstone and limestone scenery are the background to this walk to the large reservoir at Grimwith. The walking is easy, on clear tracks and field paths.

Park in a long layby at the start of a broad walled track just off the B6265 Grassington – Pateley Bridge road about half a mile east of Dibble's Bridge (GR 060 630). Coming from Grassington, Dibble's Bridge is at the foot of a very steep descent and is followed by a long pull up; the walled lane and layby are near the top on the right. Coming from Pateley Bridge the layby is on the left a few yards before a sign indicating a 1 in 6 steep hill, keep in low gear.

From the layby cross the road and go through the left-hand of two facing gates (access prohibited to motors and motor cycles) along a stony track. Soon Grimwith Reservoir, popular with windsurfers, appears ahead. Shortly after the track becomes tarmaced there are toilets and a carpark on the right. Below the carpark fork right off the tarmaced road (signposted Footpath round reservoir).

Follow the track up, soon with a wall to your left, to cross a stile by a gate. Just after the wall on the left ends, bear left off the track (footpath sign) along a well made path with the reservoir down to your left. When you reach the track again (signpost) turn left over the bridge, passing to the right of a thatched shed, and after 100 yards cross a step-stile (PF — public footpath — sign to Stump Cross) in the wall on the right.

Bear half-right on a clear path to the next stile, then continue in the same direction to pass to the right of the barn ahead and reach a ladder-stile near the corner of the field. Cross it and bear left with the PF sign, past the wall corner, but gradually bearing slightly right away from the wall (marker post with yellow top) towards a step-stile in the wall ahead. Over the stile bear half-right (signpost) and follow the marker posts across the rough pasture. Cross a broken wall and again bear slightly right (signpost) up to the next marker post, and continue parallel to the wall on your right following the posts. Pass through another broken wall and bear half-left with the posts, towards a limestone outcrop ahead, to a ladder-stile in the top left-hand corner of the field.

Cross it and the next one immediately beyond it on the left and continue round the base of the outcrop, but when the buildings of Stump Cross Caverns appear in the distance, leave the outcrop and head in their direction (the path is clear on the ground and there are marker posts). Pass a signpost at a wall corner and follow the wall on your left down to the road.

Turn right along the road, passing a long layby on the left, and go through the first gate on the left onto a stony track between broken-down stone walls. The track soon passes under power lines and soon there is a stony gully to your right. When the track forks, keep left uphill, and soon you have a wall to your right.

Follow the track up and over the crest, where there are fine views to the rocky outcrop of Simon's Seat and mid-Wharfedale. After entering a walled lane you drop to a T-junction; turn right. The lane becomes tarmaced and you drop to the hamlet of High Skyreholme.

Where the road forks after crossing Skyreholme Beck keep right on the No Through Road signposted to Parceval Hall. This fine old house is not open to the public, but the gardens can be visited. Do not cross the wooden bridge into the Hall grounds, but go through the gate a few yards before it on the left (signposted to Gill Heads and New Road).

Cross the field with the beck to your right to the facing gate and continue forward to the stile by the next gate. The track passes to the right of a barn and rises to a ladder-stile by the next gate. The track now bears slightly left and rises to pass along the left-hand side of what once must have been a mill reservoir. The limestone scenery becomes more imposing by the minute. The path contours to a stile. Walk forward, passing a footpath sign, to bear left up the dry valley along an old miners' path (the right-hand fork, along which there is no public access, leads to Trollers Gill, said to be haunted by a spectre in the shape of a large hound).

Soon there are signs of old mining activity on the left and then a stile gives access to the site of the main lead mine. A clear track leads out of the mine area again and snakes its way up the hill. It passes through a gap in the escarpment and bears left (footpath sign). Now care is needed! Where the track makes a sharp right-hand bend, keep straight ahead on a narrow path to pass to the left of a deep pothole (Hell Hole) and continue forward with a shallow ravine to the right. Soon the path bears left, passes over what look like old spoil heaps and continues forward to a ladder-stile in the wall on the right (PF sign).

Cross the road and turn left for a few yards, then cross the ladder-stile by the gate on the right. A clear green way stretches ahead with the wall to the left. Another ladder-stile by a gate leads into a walled lane which takes you back to the car.

BURNSALL AND THORPE

WALK 12

★

3½ miles (5 km) or 7 miles (11 km)

1:50 000 Sheet 98; 1:25 000 Outdoor Leisure Map 10 Yorkshire Dales
Southern Area

Clear tracks and footpaths, including one of the loveliest riverside
sections of the Dales Way make a pleasant, easy ramble. There is a
longer alternative walk. Park in the riverside carpark in Burnsall
(charge).

Walk along to the bridge, cross the road and bear right down between
the Red Lion and the bridge, turning left along the riverside path. After
half a mile you will pass Loup Scar, a large mass of limestone on the
other side of the river. The riverside path is clear to the suspension
bridge.

For the longer walk pass on to [*] on page 44.

For the shorter walk, go through a gate in the fence on the left 40
yards before the bridge (signposted to Thorpe). The path slants up to
another signpost, from where you keep straight up the slope (marker
posts), passing to the right of a telegraph pole and through a gateway in
the wall ahead (signpost). Now keep forward on the clear grassy path
parallel to the wall on the left and it will lead you over two stiles by gates
to the B6160.

Cross over and follow the minor road opposite (the hand on the old
milestone points you to Thorpe). At the top of the slope where the road
bears right to descend into Thorpe, fork left (PF — public footpath —
sign) through a gate into a walled lane. Here you are rejoined by the
longer walk.

[**] The lane turns left and descends; 20 yards before it ends at a gate
go through the gated stile in the wall on the right. Drop steeply, bearing
right parallel to the wall on the right, to a small gate at the left-hand end
of the fence ahead. Keep forward with the wood and a wall to your left.
The wall leads you to a gated stile ahead in the field corner, from where
you keep forward to cross a beck by a bridge, then bearing half-left on
the clear rising path to cross the field on a clear path to the stile in the
wall on the far side.

Follow the path forward, crossing another stile, until when you have
farm buildings down to your left you bear slightly left down to a wall,
which you then follow, keeping it on your left, to the next stile. Cross the
walled lane, then head straight up the slope towards the group of trees
on the skyline. Before you reach them the path bears slightly right and

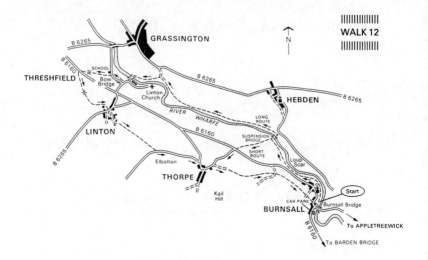

drops to a stile in the wall ahead. Now bear half-right, passing under power lines, to a stile in the bottom corner of the field.

The route is now straight across a number of fields, from one stile to the next, all the way back to Burnsall. Finally you pass through a small gate to the left of an electricity transformer and walk forward to the road. Turn right through Burnsall to return to the car.

[*] For the **longer walk**, cross the Wharfe by the bridge and immediately turn left through the stile to continue by the clear riverside path. Shortly after passing a short stretch of wall on the right, with Lythe House high above it, you go through a kissing-gate into a large pasture (the houses of Grassington can be seen ahead slightly to the right). The clear path bears slightly right away from the river, over a wooden footbridge and forward to a stile by a gate in the wall on the right.

Follow the lane past what used to be a mill on the left and a trout farm on the right, and continue to where, on a right-hand bend, there is a gap-stile on the left (signposted to Grassington Bridge). Keep forward on a clear path, with Linton church across the river on your left, crossing three stiles to enter a walled lane. Turn left over the river bridge at Linton Falls, then bear right. At a T-junction admire the packhorse bridge to your right but turn left, and at the road go left if you wish to visit the lovely mediaeval Linton church, right to continue the walk.

At the next T-junction turn right over the bridge, and just before the fine late 17th century Threshfield School go through the gate on the left and along the track with a wall to your left. Where the wall turns left keep forward on the track. Cross the old Grassington railway line by the bridge then bear slightly left on the track leading down to a gate out onto the road.

44

Go right for a few yards then through the gap-stile on the left (PF sign Linton), following the path down through the wood then straight forward over the field to a stile and clapper bridge, from which you bear slightly left to pass under power lines and under the old railway line and bear right to a gate. Keep forward across the next field, and on nearing the far side bear very slightly left to a gate in the wall ahead (PF sign). Follow the walled lane to Linton, emerging onto the road by the bridge. Turn left over this, then right along past the youth hostel on the left and a delightful packhorse bridge on the right. Linton is worth exploring: it has a wealth of fine old houses, including the 18th century Fountains Hospital beyond the green.

Follow the road forward until at the last farm you turn left (PF sign) between the farmhouse on the left and farm buildings on the right to pass through a gate and walk straight forward along a walled lane which ends at another gate, but the track continues with the wall to the left. Ignore a track turning right (signposted Cracoe) and a ladder-stile in the wall on the left and a track forking left through a gate. Follow your track until it passes through a gateway and peters out, but still keep forward along the wall on the left to a ladder-stile ahead (signpost). Keep forward on the gently rising path (noticing the fine old cultivation terraces) to pass the left-hand end of the narrow strip of woodland, then follow the wall on your right to a step-stile just to the left of the ruined building (signpost).

Turn left along the minor road and when you reach a more major road turn right into the hamlet of Thorpe. At the foot of the hill fork left and soon the road rises again out of Thorpe. Where it turns left and descends, fork right to a gate into a walled lane (signpost). Here you rejoin the shorter walk, so return to [**] on page 43.

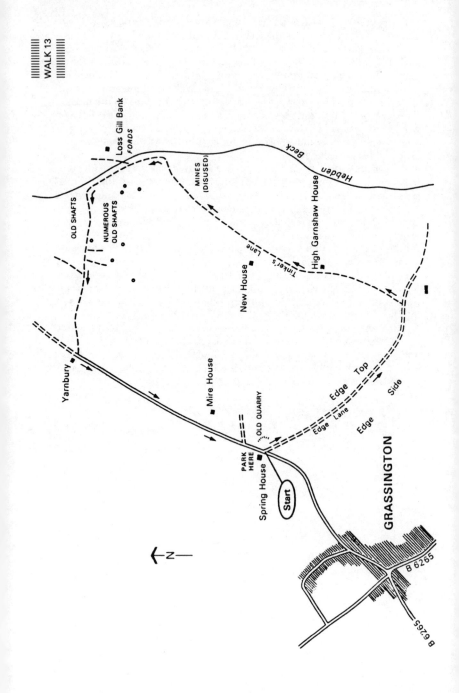

N

Loss Gill Bank
FORDS

OLD SHAFTS

NUMEROUS
OLD SHAFTS

MINES
(DISUSED)

Hebden Beck

High Garnshaw House

Tinker's Lane

New House

Yarnbury

Mire House

OLD QUARRY

PARK
HERE

Spring House

Start

Edge Top

Edge Lane

Edge

Side

GRASSINGTON

B 6265

B 6265

GRASSINGTON TO HEBDEN GILL
AND YARNBURY

WALK 13

★

4 miles (6½ km)

1:50 000 Sheet 98; 1:25 000 Outdoor Leisure Map 10 Yorkshire Dales
Southern Area

Clear tracks lead through rather bleak moorland with many remains of
the old lead-mining industry. Drive up the main street in Grassington
past the Town Hall and carry on straight up Moor Road for half a mile to
Spring House, the first large detached house on the left. Park on the
right-hand verge at a convenient spot beyond the house.

Take the walled track opposite Spring House (PF — public footpath —
sign Hebden and Hebden Gill) which gives fine views over Wharfedale
to Barden Moor and follow it to its end at a gate onto the open moor (the
former lead-mining village of Hebden is half-right below). The clear
track climbs half-left across the moor, crosses a cross-track and joins a
wall coming up from the right.
  Keep this wall on your right to a gate into another walled lane which
passes to the left of High Garnshaw House Farm. The lane bears right to
a small barn then left again, becoming a long, narrow field. Keep up the
wall on your left, passing below power lines, to a gate in the facing wall at
the top (to the left is New House Farm).
  Continue forward with the wall to your left into another walled lane.
This stretch of lane ends at a gate. Keep on down with the wall on your
right. Remains of lead-mining — spoil heaps, old buildings, a chimney
— become increasingly evident. Re-enter the walled lane, which curves
right and then left down to Hebden Beck. Pass through a gate to reach
the beckside, then turn left through another gate and follow the track
up the side of the beck. Soon the track crosses the beck for a short
distance, but the footpath doesn't.
  After the track has crossed back again it climbs through spoil heaps
before dropping to the beck again. But not for long, for soon it curves
left away from the beck again (ignore the track on the right which winds
down to recross the beck) and zigzags up the hillside. Near the top of the
slope a bridleway sign points you right through a gate. The track soon
leads you through a gateway in the wall ahead (ignore two tracks to the
left just before this) to a T-junction where you turn left. The track to the
right is the Duke's New Road, reminding us that it was the Duke of
Devonshire who developed the lead mining.
  When you reach the motor road at Yarnbury turn left along it to
return to the car.

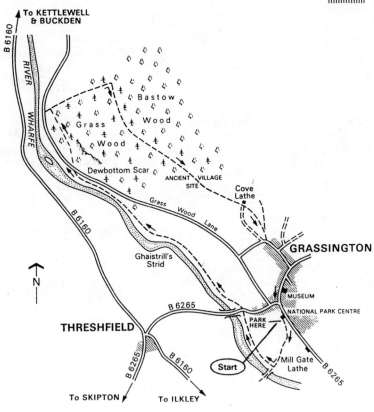

To KETTLEWELL & BUCKDEN

B 6160

RIVER WHARFE

Bastow Wood

Grass Wood

Dewbottom Scar

ANCIENT VILLAGE SITE

Cove Lathe

Grass Wood Lane

B 6160

Ghaistrill's Strid

GRASSINGTON

N

MUSEUM

NATIONAL PARK CENTRE

B 6265

PARK HERE

THRESHFIELD

B 6265

B 6160

B 6265

Start

Mill Gate Lathe

B 6265

To SKIPTON   To ILKLEY

GRASSINGTON, GRASS WOOD AND THE RIVER WHARFE

WALK 14

★

4 miles (6½ km)

1:50 000 Sheet 98; 1:25 000 Outdoor Leisure Map 10 Yorkshire Dales Southern Area

Beside the river Wharfe and through woodland, this walk can be muddy after rain and some parts of the route need careful navigation. Park in the National Park carpark in Hebden Road, Grassington (charge). The National Park Centre is worth a visit, and the village is worth exploring, perhaps with the help of the National Park's brief *Grassington Town Trail* or the more detailed *100 Things to see on a walk through Grassington*, obtainable from local shops.

On emerging from the National Park Centre bear half-left across the carpark to a gate in the wall near the bottom left-hand corner (PF — public footpath — sign Linton Falls). Turn right down the walled lane to the river. It is worth walking across the modern footbridge to admire Linton Falls beneath, but our path follows the PF sign to Grass Wood over the stile and upstream along the riverside.

Just after passing round the left-hand end of a crossing wall, bear slightly right away from the river on a clear path up to the right-hand end of Grassington Bridge. Cross the road and take the track opposite. Pass through the gate ahead (PF sign Grass Wood Lane) and follow the clear path back to the riverside. Keep to the riverside path over and through a number of stiles, including one on the left which leads you via some limestone rocks at the water's edge into a fenced path.

Eventually a ladder-stile admits you to a pasture. The river flows through a narrow channel between an island and the bank (Ghaistrill's Strid) (high on the opposite bank are two large houses). There is no clear path here, but keep forward along the riverside and you will pick one up again. Soon a step-stile leads into woodland. Shortly after this look out for a clear path climbing steeply half-right up into the woods.

A few yards after this path levels out again there is a fork, the left-hand branch descending again towards the river; keep right. From now on, all through Grass Wood, there is an abundance of paths and it is quite easy to get lost, so follow the directions closely. This route avoids all road walking. A few yards further on there is another fork, where you should keep left, in other words ignore the wide gate on the right which leads out onto the road.

Cross a cross-track and keep forward close to the wall on your right and at the next fork keep right to a stile onto the road. Cross straight over into a small carpark, but a few yards into it find a stile in the fence on the left. Cross this, turn right and follow the clear path up into the wood. Very soon you reach a T-junction; turn left on the clear cross path. Follow it to the next T-junction and here go right. At the next fork keep left. Soon you are walking parallel to the road down on the left.

The path descends gently to another T-junction; going left would lead in a few yards to the road, so go right. The track climbs gently near the edge of the wood, giving pleasant glimpses up Wharfedale. At a fork keep on the main track curving right. The track continues to climb. At a fork beside a small piece of limestone pavement keep left on the main track. Ignore all side paths and tracks, including a wide track going off left just before your track begins to descend again.

After the track has been dropping for quite some time you reach an open glade where some new trees have been planted and straight ahead is the green sign indicating the site of a Brigantian settlement dating from the 1st century AD, the time of the Roman conquest. Little more than the outlines of walls are now visible among the undergrowth.

Our path leads left out of the glade, continues to descend and leaves the wood at a ladder-stile. Cross this and walk straight across the field, bearing slightly left to a gateway (about 30 yards to the right of a barn) into a long narrow field which has two gateways close together at the far end. Walk up the right-hand edge of the field and pass through the right-hand gateway into a walled lane (Cove Lane).

Where the lane makes a sharp turn right keep straight ahead up some steps to a stile. Keep forward with the wall on your left for a few yards, then bear slightly right away from it and make for a large gap-stile in the wall on the skyline. Cross this and walk forward to enter the farmyard through a gate. Keep along the left-hand side of a long shippon (cowshed) and at the end of the buildings bear right out onto the road. Keep left along the road for the village centre.

CRACOE PINNACLE AND RYLSTONE CROSS

WALK 15

★

6 miles (9½ km)

1:50 000 Sheets 98 and 103; 1:25 000 Outdoor Leisure Map 10
Yorkshire Dales Southern Area

This is a moderately strenuous ramble, largely within the Barden Moor
Access Area, which may be closed on certain days in the grouse-shooting
season (mid-August to December), so check in advance with the
National Park Office in Grassington (tel: 0756-752774). Mostly on clear
paths and tracks, but likely to be wet in places; the walk offers excellent
views. Park in the large layby on the right just before you reach Cracoe
coming north from Skipton on the B6265 (GR 974 598).

Walk through the village using the footway on the left-hand side of the
road, and a few yards before the de-restriction sign at the far end turn
right into the tarmaced lane just after the last house on the right. When
the tarmac ends by a whitewashed house keep forward along the stony
walled lane and follow it to where it ends at a series of gates.

Pass through and bear left along the wall on your left; a final gate
leads out onto the open moor. Now look half-right, and below the crags
on the skyline you will see in the middle distance some rough hillocks
which indicate an old quarry: you are going to pass through these on the
right-hand side. At first the path keeps parallel to the wall on your left
but 20–30 yards from it, but after about 200 yards bears right up towards
the old workings. There are many paths, and it doesn't matter which one
you take as long as your general direction is correct.

Having passed behind the hillocks keep on in the same direction
slanting up the hillside and you should find yourself following a series of
parallel banks and ditches, the lines of which are marked by many loose
stones. Follow these up to where they seem to end, but in fact they curve
right, on up the hillside, with behind them a deep hollow way, which is in
fact an old track over the moors. Follow it up. It soon curves sharp left
again, then after some distance right and soon a line of low crags is
ahead of you and quite close. The hollow way leads up round the
left-hand end of the crags and continues forward over the moor to a
ladder-stile by a gate in the wall ahead.

Cross the stile and turn right alongside the wall towards Cracoe
Pinnacle, to which eventually another ladder-stile gives access. The
obelisk is Cracoe's war memorial, and a fine viewpoint. Return over the

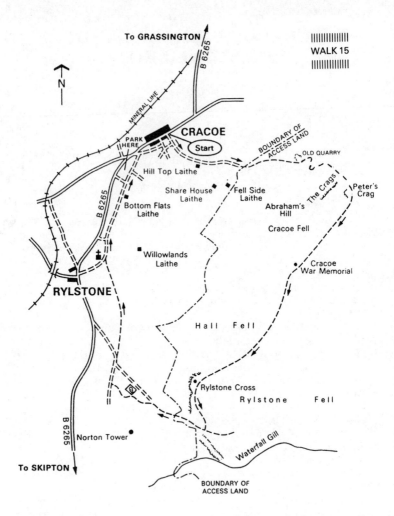

To GRASSINGTON

B 6265

MINERAL LINE

N

PARK HERE

CRACOE

Start

BOUNDARY OF ACCESS LAND

OLD QUARRY

Hill Top Laithe

Share House Laithe

Fell Side Laithe

The Crags

Peter's Crag

Bottom Flats Laithe

Abraham's Hill

Cracoe Fell

B 6265

Willowlands Laithe

Cracoe War Memorial

RYLSTONE

Hall Fell

Rylstone Cross

Rylstone Fell

Norton Tower

B 6265

To SKIPTON

Waterfall Gill

BOUNDARY OF ACCESS LAND

stile and resume your way alongside the wall on your right, soon passing an old gatepost with a deeply incised C and R, marking the parish boundary between Cracoe and Rylstone.

Eventually another ladder-stile gives access to the Rylstone Cross, erected to commemorate Queen Victoria's Golden Jubilee in 1887, and another fine viewpoint. Again return over the stile and continue following the wall on your right down. Having surmounted one last small outcrop, follow the wall down to reach a well-made gateway in it (not one of the gaps where the wall has merely collapsed) marked by a blue bridleway waymark and with a path coming over the moor from the left.

Pass through and follow the line of the old hollow way (there are marker posts), which soon becomes a clear track. Follow this clear grassy track all the way down to a walled lane. (This is not actually the line of the bridleway, which passes to the left of the wood on the way down and reaches the walled lane further to the left, but it does seem sensible to keep to the clearer track.)

Where the walled lane soon bears left, cross the ladder-stile straight ahead and bear very slightly left over the field to the next stile, then keep the same line across the next large field, heading towards the left-hand of the two woods ahead, which you enter over a gated stile by a wall-corner. Follow the wall on your left down, but where it turns right, leave the wood again by a stile ahead and walk down the next field with the wall to your left to another stile in the bottom corner. Cross over the track to the gate opposite, then bear half-right over the next field to another gate in the far corner, jumping a beck on the way.

Pass through another gate immediately to your left and walk forward towards the farm (Rylstone church is to your left), but bear right before it to pass through the left-hand of two large gates (PF — public footpath — sign to Cracoe) and walk along parallel to the fence/wall on your left. Soon a clear hollow way develops which leads to a gate into a walled lane. Keep forward and follow this back to the main road at Cracoe. Here turn left to return to the car.

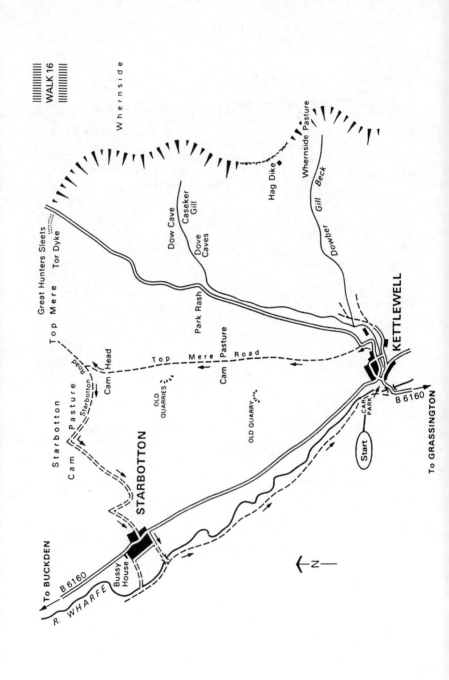

WALK 16

CAM HEAD

WALK 16

★

5 miles (8 km)

1:50 000 Sheet 98; 1:25 000 Outdoor Leisure Map 30 Yorkshire Dales Northern & Central Areas

Old tracks provide an easy walk across open moorland to a lovely stretch of riverside path (part of the Dales Way). Park in the National Park carpark (fee) in Kettlewell (on the B6160).

From the village end of the carpark by the information board follow the path to the road, turn left over the bridge by the Racehorses Hotel, then right up the village street with the beck to your right. Keep straight on at the crossroads by the post office (signposted Leyburn). The road starts to climb and makes a left-hand turn, shortly followed by a right-hand one. Leave it here and keep straight ahead on the stony walled lane (Top Mere Road — signposted Cam Head).

As you ascend, fine views open up behind down Wharfedale; the long high hill to your right is Great Whernside. After the second gate the walled lane ends; where the wall on the left turns left, ignore the track forking left and keep straight ahead on the main track. Soon you have a wall to the right, which you follow to another gate. The track is clear ahead across the open moor.

Climb gently to meet a clear cross-track at a cairn and signpost and turn sharp left (towards Starbotton). There are glorious views. Follow the track to a walled lane, and follow this down to Starbotton, soon with the deep ravine of Cam Gill Beck to your right.

On reaching the road at Starbotton, cross over and keep straight ahead down to the B6160. This hamlet has a wealth of fine houses. The Fox & Hounds is a few yards right along the main road, but our walk goes left. Opposite the last house on the left enter a walled lane on the right through a gate (PF — public footpath — signpost), keep left at the fork, and follow the lane down to the Wharfe which you cross by the new footbridge.

Turn left immediately through the gap-stile and head for another gap-stile ahead, ignoring a gate on the left. After crossing a step-stile in the fence on the left you have the river to your left, which you follow to the next gap in the wall ahead, where the path bears half-right away from the river to a step-stile to the left of the gate ahead. Bear half-right again, to cross a concrete and sleeper bridge, then left, with the river again to your left.

Follow the river until, after crossing a wooden step-stile, the path bears slightly right towards a barn. Before you reach this you are back by the river. Bear left along it, but where the river bears left keep straight ahead, crossing a sleeper bridge, then bearing slightly right to a wall corner with a ladder-stile just beyond it.

Walk forward, soon with the river to your left again and a wall to your right. Cross a step-stile and continue with the wall to your right, but where it turns sharp right keep straight on, bearing very slightly right to a ladder-stile by the next gate. Follow the wall on your right to the next ladder-stile and a clear track. Soon you are in a walled lane and now the track/path is clear back to Kettlewell. At the road turn left over the bridge to the carpark.

KETTLEWELL AND ARNCLIFFE

WALK 17

★

6½ miles (10½ km)

1:50 000 Sheet 98; 1:25 000 Outdoor Leisure Maps 30 and 10 Yorkshire
Dales Northern & Central Areas and Southern Area

This is a more strenuous ramble, involving two stiffish ascents and a
very steep descent, but the paths are clear (most of the route is
waymarked by yellow paint blobs), the views lovely, and the riverside
path in Littondale delightful. Some sections are likely to be wet. Park in
the National Park carpark in Kettlewell (fee).

Turn right out of the carpark, cross the Wharfe by the bridge and
immediately bear half-right up a stony strack to a gate (PF — public
footpath — sign Arncliffe). Walk up the short stretch of walled lane and
continue forward for 50 yards, then bear half-left up the hillside (PF
sign) on a very clear path, soon to climb steeply up a cleft in the
limestone escarpment. At the top bear half-left (yellow waymark) over
the open moor.

Can you see a wall ascending the hillside to your right? In it on the
skyline is a ladder-stile, your next objective. The path is intermittently
clear. Cross a cross-track just before a signpost and continue up the
hillside. Enjoy the views back over Kettlewell to the long ridge of Great
Whernside, then left to Buckden Pike and Upper Wharfedale. Cross the
ladder-stile and bear left parallel to the wall on your left.

On reaching the first piece of level ground after the stile, beware! The
path now forks slightly right (can you make out the waymark on the rock
100 yards ahead?) (*avoid* the left fork which seems to lead up to a gate in
the wall on the left). Having climbed through the low scar beside the
waymark, continue forward, crossing the track coming from the gate on
the left, on a very clear path. Cross another track by a spring issuing
from the hillside and keep forward on the clear path (waymark). Ahead
is another mini-scar, after which the path leads forward to cross a
ladder-stile at the watershed.

Now the descent into Littondale begins. From the stile the clear path
bears very slightly right to another stile, then half-left. On the descent
you come to a PF signpost (Arncliffe is now visible below) which
encourages you to bear slightly right. The path contours towards the
wall ahead, but before reaching it bears slightly left and descends gently
to pass through the wall. Soon you pass another signpost. The path
steepens and bears half-right to a ladder-stile; over it the descent
continues half-left. Drop quite steeply to a ladder-stile into the wood.

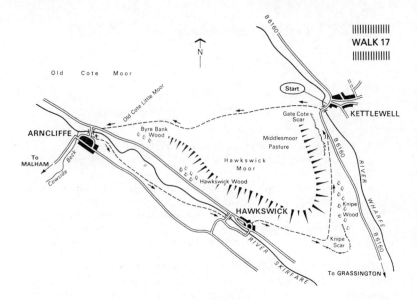

Now be careful: drop steeply forward for a yard or two, then bear left down through the scar, soon bearing right and continuing to descend steeply. Leave the wood through a gate and drop steeply to pass through a gap-stile onto the road. Cross to the stile opposite and bear right to follow the river Skirfare round to a gated stile onto the road by the bridge. Turn left over the bridge and where the road turns left keep straight ahead to the charming centre of Arncliffe.

Return to the church gate and pass through the large entrance to the right of it (PF sign Hawkswick). Walk along the drive, bearing left when you reach the big house to pass between a garage and outbuildings to a gated stile into a field. Walk forward with the fence to your right, and where it bears right keep forward, passing to the right of a power line pole with the river close by on the left. The path is clear.

Pass through a gate at the far end of the field, following the river on the left to a ladder-stile, then continuing with the wall on the left. Where the wall ends bear slightly right to a ladder-stile in the wall opposite. Follow the wall on your right to a stile in the far corner of the field. Cross the bottom of a walled lane, through the stile opposite, and walk straight forward across the middle of the next large field to a gate to the left of a barn.

Through the gate bear left round the edge of the field to a step-stile, footbridge and ladder-stile and keep straight forward across the next large field to a gate in the fence on the far side about 20 yards from the wall on the left. Then go straight forward across the next large field to a ladder-stile and on with the wall/fence and river to your left over a stile, a footbridge and another stile, continuing with the fence to your left to a step-stile at a wall corner. The river is now on your left, a wall on your right to the next stile, then the wall/fence is on your left to another step-stile and now the fence is on your right. A ladder-stile leads into a walled lane: cross the river by the footbridge.

Turn right along the road into Hawkswick. Just after Manby Barn on the left, where the road bears right, go half-left (PF sign) up the stony track to a step-stile into a walled lane. Keep forward at the junction and where the lane opens out follow the wall on your right. Soon after passing another signpost to Kettlewell the clear track bears slightly left away from the wall and climbs. Just after a gate, ignore a minor track forking left. The wall rises from the right to join you, but soon you bear slightly left away from it again. Where the green track divides, both branches bearing sharp left up the hillside, keep straight on slanting upwards, now on a much narrower path. At a fork keep left on the main path to a large cairn with a glorious view down Wharfedale.

The path now turns left by a notice admonishing you not to roll stones down the hillside and ascends to a ladder-stile in the watershed wall. Bear half-left (towards Buckden Pike in the distance), keeping at a pretty level height on a path which soon becomes clear again. The complex of buildings of Scargill House stands out down to the right. Soon you drop half-right to another large cairn.

The clear path continues to descend, crosses a ladder-stile, drops to enter a wood through a gateway in the wall beside another ladder-stile, and descends on a clear track through the wood, soon bearing left, as a path, round the bottom edge of the wood. Pass through a gap in a wall, but ignore the next gap straight ahead, bearing half-right instead to pass a small ruined building, walk forward for a few yards, then bear half-left and drop to pass through a gap in the wall on the left and follow the wall on your left down to a gate.

From the gate keep forward on the clear path through the wood, keeping left where it forks; it ascends for a few yards before dropping to the road. Turn left along the road to return to Kettlewell.

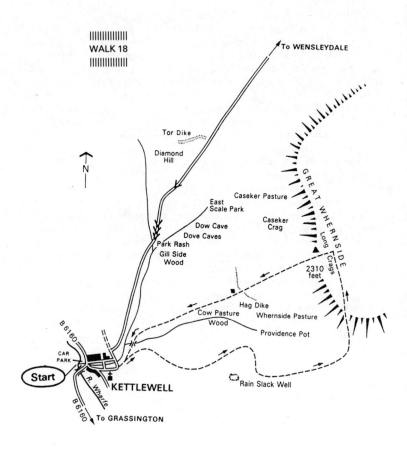

||||||||||||||
WALK 18
||||||||||||||

To WENSLEYDALE

N

Tor Dike

Diamond Hill

GREAT WHERNSIDE

Caseker Pasture

East Scale Park

Caseker Crag

Dow Cave
Dove Caves
Park Rash
Gill Side Wood

Long Crags

2310 feet

Hag Dike

Cow Pasture Wood

Whernside Pasture

Providence Pot

B 6160

CAR PARK

Start

R. Wharfe

KETTLEWELL

Rain Slack Well

B 6160

To GRASSINGTON

GREAT WHERNSIDE

WALK 18

★

6 miles (9½ km)

1:50 000 Sheet 98; 1:25 000 Outdoor Leisure Map 30 Yorkshire Dales
Northern & Central Areas

This is a strenuous, and in places wet walk, to what can be a cold and
bleak summit, but the views are superb. It must not be attempted in mist
and boots and adequate clothing are essential; take the 1:50 000 map
Sheet 98 to help identify the views from the summit. Note that there is
no right of way to the summit of Great Whernside, but access has
traditionally not been restricted. Park in the National Park carpark (fee)
in Kettlewell (on the B6160).

Turn left out of the carpark towards the village, bearing right before the
bridge then left at the maypole (signposted Leyburn, church and
police!). Past the Kings Head do not go left over the bridge but keep
straight on with the beck to your left. Shortly before the tarmaced lane
bears left over the next bridge over the beck, take the steeply ascending
track half-right (signposted Whernside Pasture).
   Pass through a gate and keep left at the fork along the wall on your left
(signpost) and where the wall ends keep forward on the clear track with
the deep ravine of Dowber Gill Beck to your left. Pass through another
gate and keep forward on the track, keeping left at the next fork, then
climbing to pass through a gate in the wall on the left. There is now a
plethora of tracks, but by keeping to the one furthest left you will be led
up to another gate in a crossing wall.
   The track continues with a wall to the left, soon entering an old walled
lane. Where this peters out go through the gateway on the left and
immediately fork right on a climbing track. It soon leads through
another gate and continues, still clear on the ground. Old mine
workings, the original reason for this track, appear ahead. Marker posts
with blue tops keep you on the right route.
   Cross a ladder-stile onto the open moor and turn right to follow the
wall on your right up (PF — public footpath — sign Capplestone Gate).
You pass to the right of a variety of cairns and keep by the wall until you
reach a large gate in it. This is where you leave the right of way. With
your back to the gate strike straight across the moor, making for the
right-hand end of the ridge of Great Whernside ahead. There is no
path, but the going is not too difficult, but take care where the grass is
tussocky and beware of drainage ditches and the bright green boggy
patches. It seems to take a long time to reach the summit ridge, but when

you do, turn left along it, parallel to the fence, and soon the going gets easier. When the fence turns right at a cairn, bear half-left (another cairn ahead marks the direction) and soon the large summit cairn is visible.

On a clear day the view from the summit (704 m, 2310 ft) is magnificent: Sheet 98 will help you to sort things out, but the Three Peaks of Pen-y-Ghent, Ingleborough and Whernside should be easily spotted.

When you are ready to move on, stand at the trig point facing the valley. Looking left, you will see a clear path heading forward towards the valley — that is your way. A row of cairns facing you some distance ahead serves as a useful marker, but the path is clear. As you descend a rather steep and eroded section you will see that there are two paths. Both lead to the cairns, but the one forking left is clearer on the ground.

From the cairns descend steeply to Hag Dike Scout Hostel, passing along to the left of the buildings to a large gate; through it, bear half-right to continue through two smaller gates with a wall on the right and fenced enclosures on the left. Pass through another gate and immediately turn right through yet another one, to follow the wall on your right along to the main entrance to the old farm on the right.

Now bear half-left across the grass (towards the trees in the valley bottom); soon you pick up a clear path which bears slightly right to pass through a gap in the wall on your right. Now watch out! Having passed through the gap, do not keep on the broad, clear path, but follow a route which bisects the angle between this path and the wall on your left (heading straight for the trees in the valley bottom). There is in fact a narrow path, which drops to cross a broken wall near the bottom left-hand corner of the field and then follows the wall on the left along to a ladder-stile. Cross this and continue with the wall to your left, and where it peters out keep forward with the steep drop to your left to a PF signpost.

Now watch out again! Follow exactly the direction of the signpost and you will bear slightly right away from the edge to drop on a clear grassy path to a ladder-stile in the next cross wall. From the stile walk forward down the slope (there is a path) to pass through a gap in a broken wall, then bear slightly right off the main grassy path to find a gap-stile in the next wall some way to the right of the gap that the main path heads for. Now bear slightly left to pick up a track which descends to a step-stile to the right of a gate. Cross and turn right beside the beck to the lane.

Turn left over the bridge, and when you reach the tarmac turn right over the bridge for an alternative route back to the car. The lane leads to a main road, where you keep straight ahead, and at the next crossroads by the post office keep straight forward to return to your starting point.

UPPER WHARFEDALE

WALK 19

★

7 miles (11 km)

1:50 000 Sheet 98; 1:25 000 Outdoor Leisure Map 30 Yorkshire Dales
Northern & Central Areas

This is an easy walk through delightful limestone scenery, with one of
the loveliest sections of the Dales Way by the river Wharfe. Park in the
National Park carpark in Buckden (GR 942 773) (fee).

Leave the carpark by the gate on the side away from the village
(signposted Buckden Pike and Cray High Bridge) and follow the clear
ascending track. When the track levels out and you reach a fork 50 yards
before a wall, keep left to the gate and signpost. Now keep forward with
the wall to your left (towards Cray High Bridge) to pass through another
gate (with a gigantic limestone gatepost) and continue with the wall to
your left on the clear grassy track. The hamlet of Cray is below left.
    A gate in the wall on the left (signposted Cray) is a short-cut to Cray,
but we continue on the level green path which is clear to the road. The
only place where you might go wrong is shortly after crossing one
ladder-stile, where you must make sure to bear slightly left to the next
one beside a gate.
    At the road turn left over Cray High Bridge and walk down to Cray.
Immediately before the White Lion Inn bear half-right (signpost to
Stubbing Bridge and Yockenthwaite), keeping on the left-hand (lower)
of the tracks, which you follow between the buildings. On emerging
from the buildings fork half-right at a small barn on the left and walk
forward to the middle one of the three gates, 20 yards to the right of a
barn (signpost). Pass through and keep forward on the clear track,
passing through another gate and keeping forward to the gap in the wall
ahead. Bear slightly right to pass a wall corner, then through a gateway
to the left of a barn, and on past another wall corner to drop gently to
cross a beck by a footbridge.
    From the bridge bear left with a wall to your left. Continue on this
grassy shelf, with fine views left down Wharfedale, until you pass round
the left-hand end of a facing wall, ascend right for a couple of yards then
continue in the same direction as before. Pass above Scar House and
follow the direction of the signpost to Yockenthwaite, i.e. bearing left to
pass through a gap-stile to the right of a gate.
    Keep forward again at the same level to pass through a gate into a
wood and follow the clear path through it, leaving it again by stiles and a
footbridge. Turn left down the fence for a few yards, then half-right on

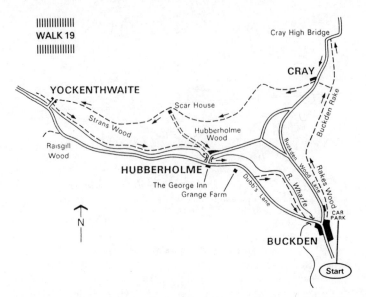

the clear path to the next gap-stile in the wall ahead. Walk forward
through two more gap-stiles, a broken wall, a wall gap (there are
frequent helpful yellow waymarks), another broken wall and another
gap-stile (yes, there is!).

Just after passing a barn some way above you on the right look out for
where the path forks left through the wall on the left (yellow waymark)
beside an ash tree. The path now slants downhill to reach another wall
by a PF (public footpath) sign: bear right along the clear path. Cross a
fence by a step-stile and keep forward to cross another stile onto a stony
track. Turn left down this to Yockenthwaite.

Fifty yards before the bridge turn sharp left on a track leading to a
gate ahead (PF sign to Hubberholme) and walk forward to a step-stile to
the left of a gate, then half-right across the corner of the field to a
gap-stile. Now bear half-left to descend to the fence by the river. Follow
the clear path, which is never far from the river, through a succession of
gates and stiles and over one footbridge to reach the church at
Hubberholme.

Walk along to the left of the churchyard wall, turning right down the
track to the road and right along the road. The charming church has a
very rare 16th century rood-loft. Cross the Wharfe by the bridge, then
turn left along the road in front of the George Inn.

Pass Grange Farm on the right, then a barn on the left, and go
through the next large gate on the left. Follow the wall on your left to the
river and bear right along the bank. Cross a stile and pass through three
gates to find yourself with a wall to your right. Where the wall turns right
keep straight ahead across the middle of the field to a gate and the road.
Turn left to return to Buckden.

WITHINS IN BRONTË COUNTRY

WALK 20

★

4 miles (6½ km)

1:50 000 Sheets 103 & 104; 1:25 000 Outdoor Leisure Map 21 South Pennines

This easy moorland walk takes clear tracks and paths to "Wuthering Heights" and the Brontë waterfalls, but some sections can be muddy. Part of the route is on the Pennine Way.

On leaving the village of Stanbury on the Haworth–Colne road there is a fork, with an island and a lamppost between the two branches: park here (GR 006 369). (If there is no room to park down at the first fork, you can drive up the left-hand branch to the next fork, again keep left and just after the tarmac ends the lane widens and there is plenty of room to park.)

Follow the left-hand branch, signposted to Top Withins and the Brontë Waterfalls. At the next fork again keep left (again signposted).

At the end of the wider section of the lane be sure to keep right, up the walled lane. Having gone through a kissing-gate by a cattle-grid you are faced with three tracks; take the right-hand one, signposted Top Withins. The Pennine Way comes along a walled lane which joins you from the right over a step-stile. Just before a long white farmhouse (Upper Heights Farm) you are joined by a track from the left; keep forward, soon bearing left to pass to the left of the farm along the clear track.

Follow the track all the way to a ruin on the right (PF — public footpath — signpost), and continue for another 200 yards to the next ruin, which is Top Withins Farm, traditionally identified with the *Wuthering Heights* of Emily Brontë's novel, although as the plaque on the wall says, it bears no resemblance to the house described in the book, although "its situation may have been in her mind when she wrote of the moorland setting of the Heights". Anyway, the view is nice!

Return the way you have come to the signpost, there forking right onto the path towards the Brontë Falls and Haworth. Follow it down, to ford a beck (this part can be muddy!), then on up the other side. Ignore a signpost pointing right to Haworth via Harbour Lodge. South Dean Beck is down in a ravine on the right. Follow the clear path, which eventually bears right down the slope to a kissing-gate: pass through for the best view of the Brontë Falls on the other side of the valley.

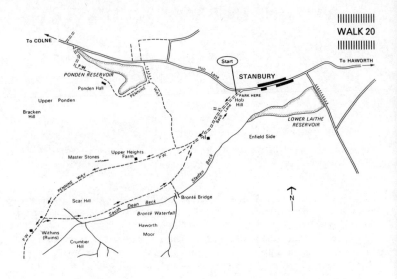

Go down to the bridge if you want, it's a lovely spot, but you will have to return up to pass through the kissing-gate again, there to fork right (signposted Stanbury and the Brontë Way). When you reach a cross-track and a facing wall, turn right towards an old barn but bear *half*-left just this side of it (ignore the path fully left) and head up to a gap-stile. The path has the remains of paving. Walk forward with a broken wall on your right to a signpost, and then keep straight forward (signposted Stanbury and Haworth); Stanbury is visible ahead, with Lower Laithe Reservoir down to its right.

Pass through an old gateway in the broken wall ahead, then keep to the left-hand side of the wall in front of you, but where this bears right keep straight on to the kissing-gate 60 yards ahead, then forward on the clear green track to emerge at the three-way junction, kissing-gate and cattle-grid you met on the way up. Turn right down the lane to return to the car.

HARDCASTLE CRAGS

WALK 21

★

6 miles (9½ km)

1:50 000 Sheet 103; 1:25 000 Outdoor Leisure Map 21 South Pennines

Estate roads, old tracks and fieldpaths provide easy walking through woodland and along a beckside past an old mill. There are fine views on the return route. From Hebden Bridge take the A6033 Haworth/Keighley road as far as a minor road on the left signposted Midgehole and Hardcastle Crags and follow this as far as the large National Trust carpark on the right opposite a lodge (small fee). Park here.

From the carpark turn right along the estate road, ignoring left and right forks in a few yards, and follow it through the woods as far as the first building on the left, Gibson Mill, a cotton mill built in 1800 and now disused. By continuing on the estate road you would reach Hardcastle Crags, but our ramble bears left through the mill-yard and crosses the bridge over Hebden Water.

Turn right immediately after the bridge. Soon you climb some steps and bear right round the old mill reservoir. Follow the clear, beckside path to the next footbridge, cross it and bear left to the next footbridge a few yards further on. Cross this one too and continue right by the beck. Soon you must jump a side beck and descend again right to the bank of the main beck. Cross the next footbridge just past a small stone building.

Follow the path going half-left up the hillside to join a level track near a little stone bridge over a small beck on the left. Turn left and follow this wide level track, ignoring a right fork just after the bridge. When you reach Overwood Cottage walk straight past it onto a contouring path. Soon you leave the wood and the clear path contours through the bracken high above the beck down on your left.

After crossing a stile the path becomes a broad level track. Soon you reach a fork: the left branch descends by some old steps to Blake Dean, a fine picnic spot where Alcomden Water flows into Hebden Water and the furthest point on our ramble. Suitably refreshed, return up the steps to the fork; facing you is again a fork: on the right the broad track by which you came, on the left an ascending path with an old stone retaining wall. Continue along the edge of the moor to a small wooden gate; pass through this, then an old gateway in the wall, then keep straight on along the wall on your left through the wood. Just after the end of the wood go through a small gate in the wall on the left and walk uphill with another wall on your left to the farm-road at New Hay Farm. Turn right along it.

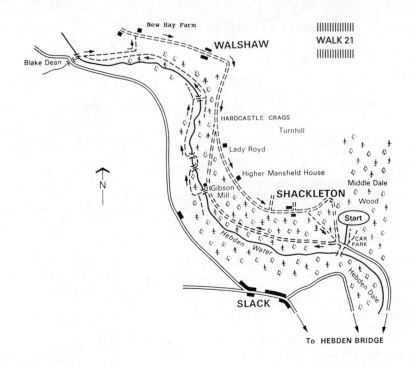

At the hamlet of Walshaw keep straight ahead ignoring forks to left and right. Shortly the road bends right to follow the curve of the valley and there is a fork. Keep left for the hamlet of Shackleton, enjoying glorious open views on the way.

From Shackleton the simpler, but longer route back to the car is to follow the road, keeping right at the junction. The more interesting route is to take the walled lane on the right just after the few houses at Shackleton and just before the next farm on the left. The bumpy grassy track leads down to a stile. Now descend the path left through the wood.

Immediately before a gap-stile turn sharp right and keep on the clear path down through the wood. It becomes less clear, but keep on in the same direction to reach a cross-track. Turn left down it (remains of causey stones) and soon you are in a walled lane which leads down to an overflow carpark. Bear right through it down a stepped path, cross the road and continue down more steps back to the car.

YORKE'S FOLLY

WALK 22

★

4½ miles (7 km)

1:50 000 Sheet 99; 1:25 000 Sheet SE06/16

This walk sets off beside the river Nidd through woodland, then out onto open moorland to Yorke's Folly, offering good views. Park in Pateley Bridge: there is a free carpark just off the High Street near the Nidd bridge; if this is full there is a carpark and picnic site at the end of Nidd Walk, the No Through Road on the town side of the Nidd bridge, from which the riverside path can be joined.

Take the riverside path (PF — public footpath — sign) to Glasshouses, passing the private bridge to Castlestead and joining the track between the mill-race and the mill reservoir to reach a road with Glasshouses Mill ahead.

Turn right and cross the Nidd. Take the left fork, then turn right past Low Fold cottages and continue up towards the wood. The track passes through a farm, skirts two more houses on the left and enters the wood by a gap-stile.

Take the right-hand path and follow it up, soon with a wire fence to the right, until it reaches a track. Turn left along the track and follow it, ignoring all paths branching left and right, as it winds up and then parallel to the long face of Guise Cliff on the right. Eventually the track climbs, giving fine views back over Nidderdale, and when you reach a wall ahead leave the main track and take the left fork up alongside the wall. Cross the ladder-stile to the left of the transmitter and bear right on the path round the back of it (Nidderdale Way sign) to follow the clear path along the top of the crags and the edge of the moor to Yorke's Folly.

The Yorke family were major landowners and leadminers in Nidderdale. It was a member of the family who had the Folly built to counter unemployment in the valley.

From the Folly follow the gently descending path across the moor to reach a sharp bend in the road at Nought Moor (PF sign). Cross the road and go through the gate; turn sharp right and follow the path over the moor to the Crocodile Rock. Can you see the likeness to the open jaws of a crocodile?

Leave the rock by the left and follow the path parallel to a wall on the right until at a bend in the wall it is joined by another path from the left.

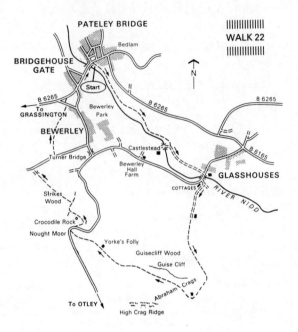

PATELEY BRIDGE

||||||||||||||||
WALK 22
||||||||||||||||

Bedlam

BRIDGEHOUSE
GATE

Start

N

B 6265
To
GRASSINGTON

Bewerley
Park

B 6265

B 6265

BEWERLEY

Castlestead

Turner Bridge

Bewerley
Hall
Farm

B 6165

COTTAGES

GLASSHOUSES

Strikes
Wood

RIVER NIDD

Crocodile Rock

Nought Moor

Yorke's Folly

Guisecliff Wood

Guise Cliff

Abraham Crags

To OTLEY

High Crag Ridge

Turn right over the ladder-stile into Strikes Wood and go downhill, then bear right down through the wood to a stile.

Do not cross this, but turn left along the edge of the wood with a wall to the right. Where the wall turns sharp right, keep straight on on the good path down to where another path comes in from the left. Here bear right downhill, parallel to a beck over on the left. Soon fork left (don't miss it!) and drop through the wood, bearing left at the foot to cross the beck by a footbridge.

Follow the wall on the left to the farm road (PF sign) and bear right over the bridge. Follow the road as far as the entrance to White Wood Farm on the left. Enter the gateway, then turn immediately sharp right over the stile (PF sign) and follow the broad path through the wood, soon leaving it to fork left to a pond and bearing left along the side of the pond.

Pass through a kissing-gate, cross a plank bridge on the right and bear left up to another kissing-gate where the wall joins the fence ahead. Turn right up the wall-side (steps) and continue to a gap-stile in the field corner ahead. Walk straight down the next large field to the bottom right-hand corner, to pass through a gap in the broken wall and follow the wall on the right to the road.

Turn left along the road to find a gap-stile on the right immediately after crossing the beck. Walk parallel to the beck for a few yards before bearing left up towards a streetlamp behind the hedge. Cross the stile onto the B6265 opposite Hill Top Farm and turn right down this busy road (care!) back to Pateley Bridge.

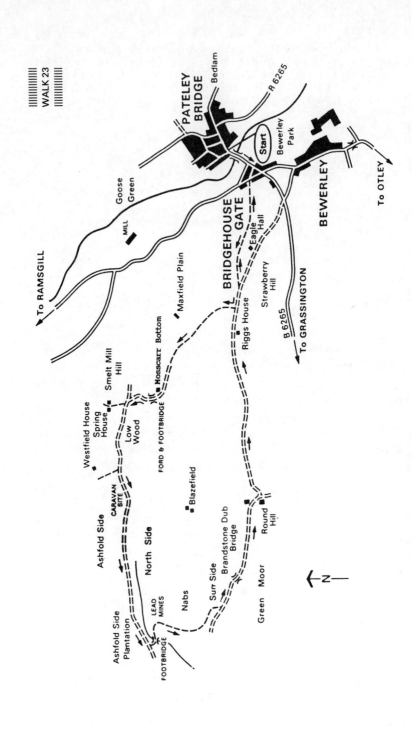

WALK 23

To RAMSGILL

PATELEY BRIDGE

Bedlam

B 6265

Goose Green

MILL

Start

Beverley Park

BRIDGEHOUSE GATE

Maxfield Plain

Eagle Hall

BEWERLEY

Strawberry Hill

Riggs House

To OTLEY

B 6265

To GRASSINGTON

Smelt Mill Hill

Westfield House

Spring House

Mosscarr Bottom

Low Wood

FORD & FOOTBRIDGE

CARAVAN SITE

Ashfold Side

North Side

Blazefield

Ashfold Side Plantation

LEAD MINES

Nabs

Brandstone Dub Bridge

Sun Side

FOOTBRIDGE

Green Moor

Round Hill

N

MOSSCARR AND ASHFOLD BECK

WALK 23

★

5 miles (8 km)

1:50 000 Sheet 99; 1:25 000 Sheet SE06/16

Field-paths and tracks take the walker through a moorland valley and visit an old lead-mine. Park in Pateley Bridge (see Walk 22).

Cross the Nidd bridge and just past Nidderdale Motors and before Park View Stores take the ginnel (narrow alley) on the right. At the next road turn right for a few yards before taking the first lane on the left between houses. Follow it to a white gate with a kissing-gate beside it and keep straight up the next field close to a wall on the left, and go through a gate with a barn on the right.

Now keep close to a hedge on the left, go through a gate with steps (NOT the gate into Eagle Hall grounds), and then head straight on with the wall/hedge on the left to a kissing-gate and then a step-stile on the left in the top corner of the field. Bear right through the tiny wood to a lane.

Turn right along the lane until you reach a gate on the right in the wall at the beginning of a small wood. Go through the gate, and another in a few yards, then continue with a hedge on your right to pass through a gate in the wall ahead. Follow the wall on the left down and round, through a gateway and on to a facing gate in the next field corner. Cross the next field to another gate (aim for the next farm ahead) and follow the wall on the right to another gate and a walled lane.

Follow it down to a footbridge near the house at Mosscarr Bottom. Over the bridge turn right up another walled lane, passing through a gate at its end and bearing right down the next rough lane towards a caravan site. Cross Ashfold Side Beck by the bridge and turn left when through the gate.

Follow the track up the valley, passing through Westfield Caravan Site (over the cattle grid). Beyond this the track sometimes rises high above the beck. Eventually you will see across the beck the remains of a huge lead mine with large spoil heaps. Our route follows the path that leaves the high track (Nidderdale Way sign) and heads down to go through a gate and cross the beck by a large concrete slab near a ruined mill building. (This gate is clearly seen from the top track if you should happen to go too far along it.)

After crossing the beck bear left up the well-defined hillside track, but in a few yards (Nidderdale Way sign) double back above the old buildings and follow the clear path up between the spoil heaps. At a wall corner the path veers left, roughly following the wall, then, after crossing near the top of the workings, winds round right, passing between a solitary tree on the left and a fragment of building on the right. Soon you are on a good track.

Pass through a large gateway and continue along the track. At the first junction keep straight on (Nidderdale Way sign) and at the next fork keep right (another sign) down to Brandstone Dub bridge across the beck. Bear left with the track after the bridge, soon to join a walled lane. At the second farm follow the track sharp left.

Now follow this road, ignoring tracks left and right, to breast the hill and descend past Riggs House (on your right) to reach the tiny wood which you came through on the outward journey. Bear left through it once more and retrace your steps to Pateley Bridge.

MIDDLESMOOR AND HOW STEAN

WALK 24

★

7 miles (11 km)

1:50 000 Sheet 99; 1:25 000 Sheet SE07/17

This is a gentle ramble through the lovely scenery of Upper Nidderdale, mainly on clear tracks and field paths. Part of the walk is on the Nidderdale Way. Do make time to explore Middlesmoor, a proud hilltop village of charm and character. (There are public toilets beside the Crown Hotel.)

Park in Middlesmoor carpark at the head of Nidderdale; the carpark is near the top end of the hamlet, shortly before the tarmac ends, on the right (GR 092 743). Enjoy the view from the carpark before setting off.

On leaving the carpark turn left, then before the first house left again, then immediately left again through a gap-stile, to walk back past the carpark to the next gap-stile on the other side of the field. Keep forward with the wall on your left to another stile, then on to another one, then bear right round the edge of the wood, following the fence, and where the wood ends keep straight forward across the middle of the field to a gap-stile in the wall ahead.

Keep forward, crossing the farm access track and passing to the left of Smithfield Hall Farm, before bearing slightly left (the path is clear) to the next stile. Walk straight over the next field to another stile, then slightly left to the next stile in the wall on the left. Turn right along the lane, passing to the left of Northside Head Farm, and follow the track until you reach a gate by the corner of a wood on the left.

Through it turn immediately right over a stile by another gate and bear slightly left down the field, bearing more sharply left shortly before the trees to ford a beck, then half-right to a stile in the wall on the right in the field corner. Bear half-left across the next field to a step-stile 15 yards to the right of the field corner, then slightly left to the next stile in the wall on the left. Now go half-right down the next field (clear path) to a stile some way to the left of a solitary oak, then straight down the next field to a gap-stile onto the road.

Cross straight over to another stile, then down the next field to a gate to the left of a barn, keeping forward to another gap-stile onto the farm access road, no doubt accompanied by the barking of the many (chained) dogs, and turning right along it. Where it bears right, keep forward (Nidderdale Way sign) to a stile by a gate, then bear left along the fence on the left (another signpost) to a stile in it.

Now keep forward on the clear path with the river bed to your left,

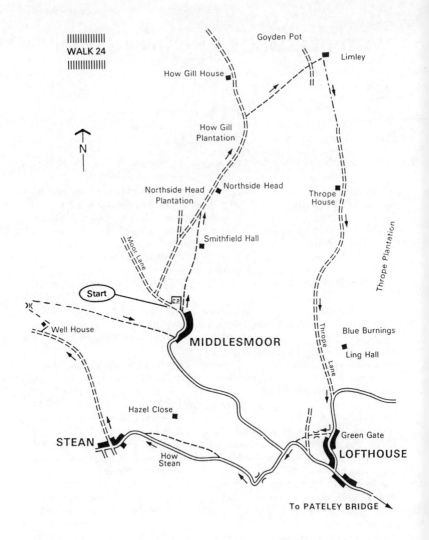

soon crossing a ladder-stile in the fence on the right and bearing left along this fence until you cross another ladder-stile in it and bear right across the river bed onto an old track with the remains of a wall to your left. Soon you bear left away from the river in what was once a walled lane. It leads to Thrope Farm, passes to the left of it and continues as a walled lane.

The track is clear all the way to the next road, where you keep forward down into Lofthouse. At the war memorial, where the road turns left, keep right along a stony track, and follow it until it bears left to cross the

Nidd by a stone bridge. Pass through a gap-stile and walk forward to cross a minor road, pass through a kissing-gate and follow the boundary fence of the cricket ground on your left, bearing slightly right after the barn to another kissing-gate by a large gate (PF — public footpath — sign).

Bear right along the road, forking left in 100 yards into a No Through Road signposted to Stean only, and follow it up to the hamlet of Stean, passing on the way the entrance to the spectacular How Stean Gorge, which can be visited (charge); here there is also a café.

Ignore the first PF sign to Middlesmoor at the approach to Stean, continue past the telephone kiosk, follow the road round a sharp right-hand bend, then take the lane on the right in front of some cottages over a cattle-grid marked Stean Farm: Private Road (don't worry, there is a right of way!). The track passes between the farmhouse on the left and the farm buildings on the right, through a gate and over another cattle-grid. In 60 yards keep right at the fork and follow the track to Well House, the next large house on the right.

As you approach Well House look out for a waymark in the fence on the right pointing you through a gate and along a fenced path to another gate. Pass the right-hand end of the buildings to another gate, then bear half-left on a clear grassy path which descends to another gate at the side of the beck. Through this it is easiest to bear right to cross the beck where it is narrow, then bearing left along the side of the beck, but the right of way actually goes forward for a yard or two from the gate then bears left to slant across the beck over the slabs, a route which can be wet and slippery. In both cases you must follow the far bank of the beck left until you are faced by a side beck coming from the right. Cross this where it joins the main beck and bear right steeply up for a yard or two to find an old stone bridge, with an old limekiln to the left on the nearside, leading right back over this side beck.

The clear path now bears half-right, with trees to the right, before slanting gently up into the trees on the left. When you have a wall close by on the left, ignore a path going left up to a gate in it and keep forward up to a step-stile in the fence on your left. Ascend a clear path through the bracken, and when you reach the grass keep forward, heading towards a barn, to pass through a gap in the fence ahead. Now bear slightly right, to the right-hand end of the wall coming down from the barn, to pass through a gap-stile and continue forward with a fence and old hedge to your left.

The fence kinks left and right, but you keep straight ahead to a gap-stile in the wall in front a few yards to the left of a gate. (The waymark has got onto the gatepost instead of onto the stile!) Through the stile bear slightly left to a gateway in the wall ahead. Pass through and follow the track along with a fence to your right, to a gate. Pass round to the right of the barn, through two gates, and walk forward on the track to the road in Middlesmoor opposite the Wesleyan Chapel.

Walk along to the right of the chapel, bearing right at the cobbled street and along to the churchyard gate (ignoring a PF sign to Lofthouse on the right). Inside the churchyard bear right down to the war memorial where there is a bench with one of the best views in the locality. Leave the churchyard again by the same gate and bear right up the tarmaced path, cross a track and keep forward, up with a handrail to your left, bearing left at the top to a little green, then left again to the main road near the Crown Hotel. Turn right up the road to return to the car.

MIDDLESMOOR AND SCAR HOUSE

WALK 25

★

7 miles (11 km)

1:50 000 Sheet 99; 1:25 000 Sheet SE07/17

This walk is a delightful exploration of Upper Nidderdale, mainly on clear tracks and field paths with fine views. Much of the route is on the Nidderdale Way. Park in Middlesmoor carpark (see Walk 24).

Turn right out of the carpark, follow the tarmac to its end and continue up the stony track (In Moor Lane), ignoring a track forking right a short distance up.

Enjoy the views back down Nidderdale as you ascend. Opposite a small Yorkshire Water building on the right, notice an old milestone on the left, now illegible: this was once the road over to Coverdale. After the walled lane ends, a clear track continues over the moor. Follow it all the way to Scar House Reservoir. The view extends from Great Whernside over to the left, via Little Whernside to Dead Man's Hill ahead.

Turn right along the tarmaced road, but soon bear left over the reservoir dam; a plaque tells you that the reservoir, which supplies water to Bradford, was opened in 1936. At the far side of the dam bear half-left up the stony track, in 100 yards turning sharp right onto a signposted grassy bridleway (and Nidderdale Way). Cross a track coming up from the house down on the right. Through a gate keep right at a fork, i.e. straight ahead on the main track.

Passing through a gateway, briefly you have a wall on the right, and the quality of the track deteriorates. When the wall ends keep straight ahead over a footbridge. Soon you pass through another gate and to the left of a small wood. When faced by a ravine, the track winds down, crosses a beck by a bridge, climbs steeply, fords another beck and continues to climb. About 150 yards before a flat-roofed shooting-house look out for a track forking right by a white topped marker post. Follow this track, marked by a line of posts, down to pass through a gate in the wall on your right.

The track bears right downhill, soon turning sharp left parallel to a wall on the right. Pass through a gate in a fence, and another in a wall, to reach a Nidderdale Way sign pointing back the way you have come. Now the track follows the wall on the left. Pass through another gate, keep left at a faint fork by a solitary hawthorn (i.e. stay on the main track) and pass under telegraph wires to a wall corner and another Nidderdale Way sign.

Turn sharp right on the descending track, soon with a beck on your

79

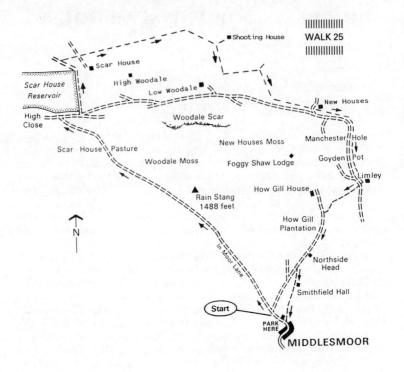

left, and soon bearing left to pass through a gate, then slightly right across the next field to pick up a wall which you follow on your left to a gate. Keep the wall to your left and the river Nidd to your right until you reach the access road at New Houses (river bridge to right).

Turn left over the cattle-grid, fork right in a few yards over another one and bear right along to the left of some buildings to a gate on the left at the far end. Keep on in your previous direction to pick up a wall to your left, which becomes a fence, which you follow until you reach a gate by the river. Keep the river on your right to another gate and then keep forward, there is no path, to a stile in the fence on your right halfway along the field.

Cross the footbridge and turn left along the edge of the field until you reach a gap-stile in the wall at the far end. Cross it and walk forward to the step-stile into the next field. Keep along the bottom of the slope on your right, passing a solitary hawthorn. The stile high in the fence on your right gives access from the road above to Manchester Pot down on your left, where the Nidd disappears underground, to re-emerge near Lofthouse. You reach a track, which you follow with a fence to your left.

80

The track soon advances to pick up the fence on your right, but where the clear track ends keep forward along the fence on your left, passing a stile in it which gives access to Goyden Pot, another swallow hole, and continuing by the dry river bed until you are forced right by a side beck. In a few yards bear left to cross it and keep forward, with a wall on your right, to a gate at Limley Farm.

Keep bearing right through the farmyard (with many noisy, chained dogs!), passing through another gate on the right and walking forward to yet another one, then crossing over the middle of the field to a gap-stile onto the road.

Now you return to Middlesmoor by the outward route of Walk 24. Cross straight over to another gap-stile, straight up the next field to the next one, and now half-left to the next one. Now bear right round the edge of the next field to a step-stile a few yards left of the corner, then slightly left to the next stile just to the left of a tree. Your next target is the left-hand end of the wood up ahead, so first bear half-left, ford the beck and make your way steeply up to a stile by a gate in the top corner of the field.

Cross it and turn immediately left through another gate. The view opens up left down Nidderdale to Gouthwaite Reservoir. Follow the track past Northside Head House, then 40 yards before the wood on the right ends, cross a gap-stile in the wall on the left, bear half-right to the next one, then straight ahead to the next one. The clear path continues forward, passing to the right of Smithfield Hall Farm and crossing the access track, to the next gap-stile in the wall ahead. Keep on towards the right-hand end of the wood ahead, pass round it, through two more stiles, then on with the wall on your right to another stile. Walk straight forward across the next field passing two wall corners on the right (with your car behind) to a gap-stile in front of the end of the building ahead. Turn right to the road and right to your car.

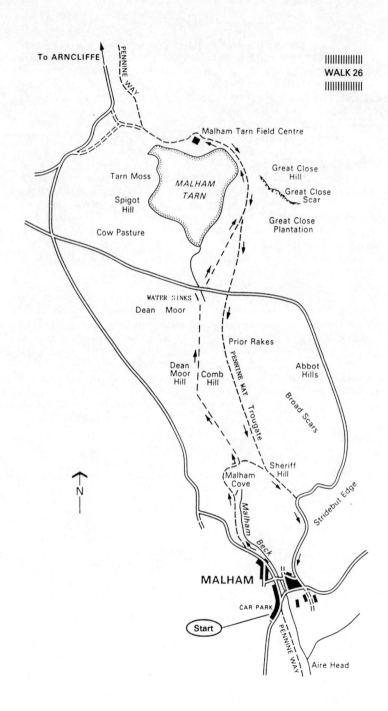

To ARNCLIFFE

PENNINE WAY

IIIIIIIIIIII
WALK 26
IIIIIIIIIIII

Malham Tarn Field Centre

Tarn Moss

MALHAM TARN

Great Close Hill

Great Close Scar

Spigot Hill

Cow Pasture

Great Close Plantation

WATER SINKS

Dean Moor

Prior Rakes

Abbot Hills

Dean Moor Hill

Comb Hill

PENNINE WAY

Trougate

Broad Scars

Malham Cove

Sheriff Hill

Stridebut Edge

N

Malham Beck

MALHAM

CAR PARK

Start

PENNINE WAY

Aire Head

MALHAM COVE AND TARN

★

6 miles (9½ km)

1:50 000 Sheet 98; 1:25 000 Outdoor Leisure Map 10 Yorkshire Dales Southern Area

Partly on the Pennine Way, this walk passes through spectacular limestone scenery and skirts Yorkshire's largest lake. The route includes a section of very steep path (but it is well made and there is no sense of exposure) and some walking over limestone, which can be slippery after rain. This is a very popular area and can be busy in summer and at weekends.

Park in the National Park carpark on the edge of Malham village (charge). A visit to the adjacent Information Centre is worthwhile, and there are toilets.

Turn left out of the Information Centre and left again along the road through Malham. Where the road forks keep left, and look out for a telephone kiosk on the right: just beyond it is a small gate into woodland (Pennine Way signpost). Soon you rejoin the road and turn right. After leaving the village the road begins to climb. Follow it to a gate on the right (Pennine Way sign) and then follow the clear path to Malham Cove.

Shortly before you reach the Cove, notice a clear path forking left and climbing steeply to the top of the Cove by steps. That is your route, after you have walked forward to have a look at the bottom of the cliff face itself.

From the top of the steep path cross either of the ladder-stiles in the facing wall and bear left up to a shelf in the limestone pavement. Here bear right (Pennine Way sign) across the full width of the pavement, taking care on the broken, uneven and slippery surface (the going is easier further up the slope to the left where there is more grass). When you reach the facing wall on the far side you leave the Pennine Way (which crosses the wall) and turn left, keeping the wall on your right, up the dry valley known as the Watlowes. Soon you enter the National Trust's Malham Tarn Estate.

The valley narrows and you climb a stepped path which leads you through a gap in the wall on your right and forward to a stile. Over this bear sharp right, still on a clear path (signpost to Water Sinks and

Malham Tarn). The path soon bears left and leads up another dry valley. Shortly you have a wall to your right. For a brief stretch the path becomes uncomfortably stony, then changes to a grassy carpet.

Pass a ladder-stile in the wall on the right, with a signpost pointing back the way you have come, and keep forward, now about 20 yards to the left of the wall, to Water Sinks, where Malham Water disappears underground, to emerge again at Aire Head, south of Malham village, and become the river Aire. Now bear half-left away from the beck to a footpath signpost, and then slightly right to a gate onto the road.

Turn right along the road, crossing Malham Water, to reach a carpark on the left. Turn left along the near edge of this to the back where there is a shallow ditch. Three short wooden posts mark the start of a bridleway, a grassy track, which bears slightly right away from the carpark. The track is clear across the moor and soon Malham Tarn is visible left. The track passes to the right of a small wood and continues forward to meet an unsurfaced road a few yards before a gate. Here you rejoin the Pennine Way.

Go left along the road, through the gate into the Malham Tarn Nature Reserve. Walk along this road, which soon reaches the shore of the Tarn before entering woodland and leading to Malham Tarn House (a Field Studies Centre) as far as you want and then retrace your steps to the gate. About 20 yards beyond the spot where you joined this road, another faint track leaves it on the right at an angle of about 30 degrees, soon becoming clear on the ground. This is the Pennine Way. It leads to the tarmaced road about 200 yards to the left of the carpark you crossed on the outward route.

Walk straight over the road (Pennine Way sign) and continue up the gently rising track opposite. It leads to a ladder-stile in a crossing wall and over that bears slightly left to a signpost marking a crossing of paths. Here keep straight on towards Malham Cove. The clear grassy track leads over the brow of the hill to another ladder-stile in a crossing wall beside another National Trust sign.

Keep forward on the clear track, uncomfortably stony for a short distance, pass through a gap in the next crossing wall and continue forward on a track which is now almost a hollow way. Malham Cove is down to your right. Cross the next wall by a ladder-stile and keep forward. (The Pennine Way comes up from the Cove at this point.) Pass a signpost some yards to the left of a wall and keep forward on the clear track, with the wall to your right for a short distance, to reach the road by another stile.

Turn right down this Malham Rakes road to return to the village. When you reach the first house on the right, bear right down the track (in front of a large sycamore surrounded by a wall). Where, in a few yards, the track appears to fork, keep left, down between houses, and at a T-junction go left again on a tarmaced lane, down past the youth hostel. At the main road turn right past the Listers Arms, cross the bridge and bear left to the car.

JANET'S FOSS AND HANLITH

WALK 27

★

5½ miles (8½ km)

1:50 000 Sheet 98; 1:25 000 Outdoor Leisure Map 10 Yorkshire Dales
Southern Area

This walk follows field paths to a waterfall in spectacular limestone
scenery, crosses moorland with fine views and returns along a delightful
riverside path. The area is very popular so it is busy in summer and at
weekends. Park in the National Park carpark on the edge of Malham
village (see Walk 26).

From the carpark turn left past the Information Centre and left again
along the road through the village until just before the Sparth House
Hotel. Here cross the road, pass to the right of a cottage, over a clapper
bridge and turn right along the track (signpost Pennine Way, Janet's
Foss, Gordale Scar). Cross a step-stile and continue on the path by the
beck to a ladder-stile, and straight on over the middle of the field to pick
up a wall on your left which you follow to the next ladder-stile.

Now the route couldn't be easier: follow this delightful, clear, made
path all the way to Janet's Foss.

Keeping the waterfall down on the right, ascend the clear path to a
kissing-gate and the road. Turn right. After crossing Gordale Beck by a
bridge the road bears right and on the left is a small gate and a sign to
Gordale Scar. Here a detour to inspect the Scar is a must, before
retracing your steps to the road.

Continue up the road; there are fine views back. Almost at the top of
the hill take the walled lane on the right (signposted Calton) and climb it
to its end at Weets Cross. After pausing to enjoy the views go through
the gate. The trig point on Weets Top at a height of 1,357 feet is a few
yards to the left, and a footpath signpost is just in front of you.

Follow the clear track going straight forward; it soon bears slightly
right, and shortly you are walking parallel to the wall on your right about
30 yards away. When the track brings you quite close to the wall there is a
crossing of paths: follow the signpost to Hanlith, which takes you over to
the wall and across a ladder-stile. Marker posts with yellow tops now
point the way forward. First you walk parallel to the wall on your left —
the path is clear on the ground — but soon the path leads you slightly
right away from the wall across the moor.

Having crossed the moor you pass through a gate into a walled lane.
There are views over to Malham on the way down. The lane brings you
to Hanlith. (At the beginning of the hamlet the Pennine Way comes in

85

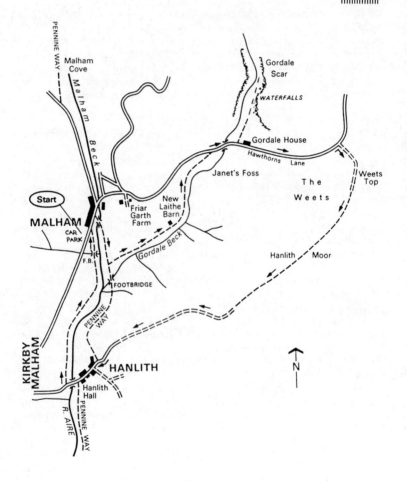

Start

MALHAM
CAR PARK

PENNINE WAY

Malham Cove

Malham Beck

Malham Cove

Gordale Scar

WATERFALLS

Gordale House

Hawthorns Lane

Janet's Foss

Friar Garth Farm

New Laithe Barn

F.B.

Gordale Beck

FOOTBRIDGE

PENNINE WAY

The Weets

Weets Top

Hanlith Moor

KIRKBY MALHAM

HANLITH

Hanlith Hall

PENNINE WAY

R. AIRE

N

from the right on a sharp left-hand bend.) Notice the bronze of St Francis in the wall of a house on the right opposite Hanlith Hall on the left. Cross the Aire by the road bridge and turn right along the minor road by the river. There now follows a lovely stretch of riverside walking.

When you reach Scalegill Mill go through the small kissing-gate to the left of the main entrance and follow the path round the side of the buildings. Then continue on the clear path by the mill goit. After crossing a step-stile you have a wall to your right. Just before the gated stile in the next facing wall and again just after it springs on the right are the official sources of the river Aire (Aire Head).

Continue across the field to a ladder-stile beside a gate in the far wall. Cross this and walk straight forward over a footbridge and along to the next ladder-stile in the field corner. Over this keep forward on the clear path to reach Malham village over another ladder-stile to the left of a gate in the far wall of the field. Turn left to return to the car.

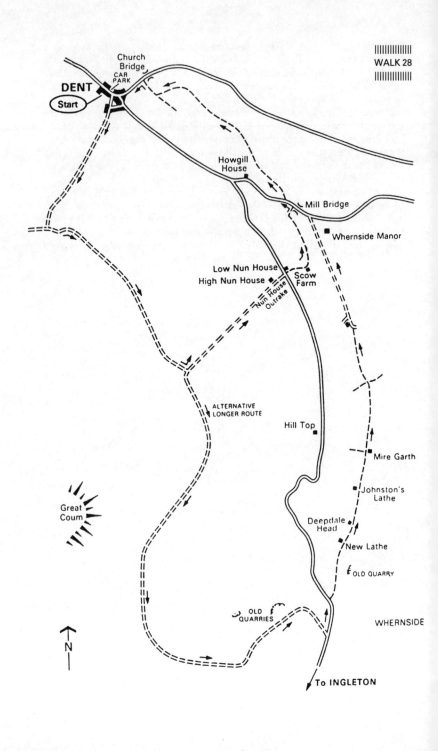

WALK 28

PANORAMA WALK FROM DENT

WALK 28

★

10 miles (16 km) or 4½ miles (7 km)

1:50 000 Sheet 98; 1:25 000 Outdoor Leisure Map 2 Yorkshire Dales
Western Area

Panoramic views of Dentdale, the Howgill Fells and Whernside, and a
stretch of riverside along part of the Dales Way are the rewards on this
ramble. There are some delightful field paths but a long contouring
bridleway can be very muddy. There is a shorter alternative walk. Park
in the National Park carpark in Dent village (small charge).

On leaving the carpark turn left for a few yards, then right up the road
to the left of Dentdale Memorial Hall. Pass to the right of the village
green and keep straight on up a No Through Road unsuitable for
motors. Where the tarmac ends a signpost points straight ahead to
Flintergill. Ascend the steep, stony, but attractive track with the ravine
of Flintergill to your left.

When you reach a gate and T-junction turn left along the walled lane.
Now the panorama opens up, from the Howgill Fells behind you to the
left, up the length of Dentdale to Great Knoutberry Hill at its head and
round to Whernside. Eventually you cross a beck to reach another
T-junction.

For the **shorter alternative walk** go left here (signposted Nun House
and Outrake) (see [*] on page 91).

For the **main walk** go right (signposted Whernside). Follow this
walled lane, which can be very muddy, all the way to the next road; at
one point the walls peter out, but the track is clear on the ground, at
others there is only a wall or fence on one side of it. There is only one
track which forks left out of the lane, and it should be ignored.

When you reach the road turn left down it. Over the brow of the hill
there are splendid views of Deepdale. Just after a slight left-hand bend
cross a ladder-stile (PF — public footpath — sign to Mire Garth) on the
right and follow the clear path downhill (marker posts with white tops
point the way). Now follows the only section where care should be taken
with route finding. On reaching another PF sign bear left down a raised
bank to another ladder-stile and continue downhill with a fence, then a
beck and a line of trees, to your left.

Cross the concrete track and walk down with the farm (Deepdale
Head) to your left to a large gate into the farmyard, where you bear right
to a smaller gate leading to a bridge over the beck. Bear left along the
beck, pass to the right of a small stone barn and bear slightly left on the

track towards the valley bottom, but again after a few yards bear slightly right on a narrow path to pass through a gap in the line of trees ahead.

Cross the side beck and bear slightly left to pass to the right of a barn, then continue forward to pass through a gap-stile in the facing wall a few yards to the left of the next barn. Bear slightly right past the wall corner and head for a gap in the wall in the far right-hand corner of the field. Continue parallel to the wall on your right to the next farm (Mire Garth).

Just before the farm you cross a beck by a stone bridge; pass to the left of the buildings on the concrete track, turning right at the far end of the garden wall for a few yards then left along with the wall to your right. Cross a gap-stile in the field corner and keep on with the wall/fence to your right. Cross a beck and a stile, pass to the left of a derelict farm and keep forward with the wall to your right. Cross a gap-stile and another side beck and continue with the wall to your right.

Where the wall turns right keep straight forward to pass to the left of the next barn (although the clearer path passes to the right of it), bearing left down with the beck to your right to cross a ladder-stile on the other side of the beck about 40 yards down from the barn. Bear very slightly left across the next field on a clear path, parallel to Deepdale Beck to your left. Soon you have a steep drop to cross another side beck just to the right of a wooden telegraph pole.

Walk straight over the next field parallel to the beck on the left; cross another side beck, then bear half-right to a stile at the left-hand end of the wall ahead. Cross this and walk forward with the wood to your left to a stile in the corner beside a large conifer. Continue forward with the wall to your right through a gateway into a walled lane. Turn left along it. Now the route finding is easy again.

Follow the lane straight through the next farmyard and continue in it (enjoying the species-rich old hedges) all the way to the next main road. Here turn left. When you reach the next house on the right ignore the stile and PF sign to Tommy Bridge, cross the road bridge and in a few yards bear right down the path signposted to Church Bridge.

[**] You are now on the Dales Way. Follow the clear path, at first beside Deepdale Beck, then beside the river Dee, all the way to Church Bridge. As you approach the bridge, the path bears left away from the river, passes to the left of a ruined building, crosses a concrete bridge and then bears right along with a beck to the right. At the bridge turn left up the road to return to Dent village and your car.

' [*] **Shorter alternative walk:** Having turned left at the T-junction, follow the walled lane down to the road, passing to the right of High Nun House Farm near the bottom. Cross straight over and walk down the path with a wall to your left (signposted Millbridge), crossing a track by gates (PF sign) and continue forward to another gate ahead. Through this, follow the right-hand edge of the field down, bearing right at the bottom along the track to a gate. Ahead is Scow Farm.

Through the gate turn immediately left (PF sign) down to a stile by the corner of the house. Cross it and walk forward across the middle of the next field (marker post) to a stile in the wall on the far side. Pass an old lime-kiln on the left, then bear left to pass through the line of trees on the left, then follow this line to where it ends by a large ash, there bearing slightly left to the next stile in the wall ahead.

Keep forward, passing about 30 yards to the right of a small stone shed and slanting gently down to the line of trees at the bottom of the field. A yellow waymark and the remains of a stone gap-stile indicate where you pass through the line of trees and drop on a clear path to the side of Deepdale Beck. Bear left to a gate onto the road. Turn left for a few yards, then right along the clear path signposted to Church Bridge. You have now rejoined the route of the main walk, so return to [**] above.

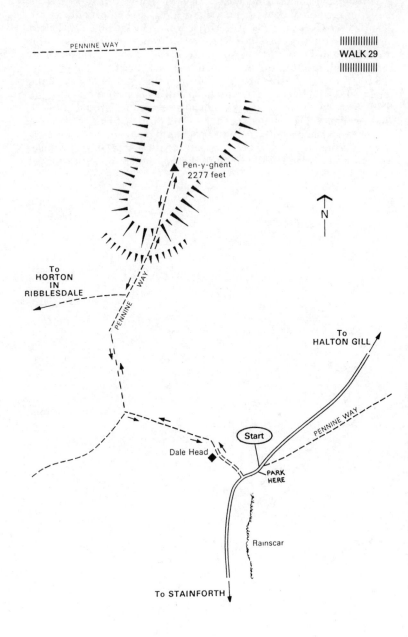

PENNINE WAY

||||||||||||
WALK 29
||||||||||||

Pen-y-ghent
2277 feet

To
HORTON
IN
RIBBLESDALE

PENNINE WAY

N

To
HALTON GILL

PENNINE WAY

Start

PARK
HERE

Dale Head

Rainscar

To STAINFORTH

PENYGHENT

WALK 29

★

3½ miles (5½ km)

1:50 000 Sheet 98; 1:25 000 Outdoor Leisure Map 2 Yorkshire Dales
Western Area

This short walk to a superb viewpoint is easy except for one brief but
very steep ascent (and the corresponding very steep descent).

From Settle drive up the B6479 Horton in Ribblesdale road as far as
Stainforth, there forking right (signposted Halton Gill and Arncliffe).
Cross the bridge in the centre of the village and keep straight on
(signposted Arncliffe). Once out in the country ignore a right fork (to
Malham) and park beside the road just after the first cattle-grid (GR 843
714).

From here the whole course of the walk to the summit of Penyghent is
visible: notice the wall ascending from the left of the hill up to the right
of the nose and the eroded path to the right of the wall — that is your
route up. The entire walk is on the Pennine Way.

Return over the cattle-grid, where there is an information board, and
go through the first gate on the right (signposted Pennine Way:
Penyghent) and follow the access road to Dale Head Farm. When you
reach it bear right to pass the nearside end of the barn and follow the
track through a gate. The track continues to a ladder-stile by the next
gate, and should now be followed to a fork. Here keep right on a new,
well-made path (signposted Penyghent), part of a large scale National
Park project to combat erosion in the Three Peaks Area. The route up to
the summit becomes increasingly clear. When the new path ends it is
only a short distance to a ladder-stile in the wall on your right.

Over this, follow the wall on your left, ascending the hill by the badly
eroded path and keeping forward to the trig point on the summit (the
wall is an infallible guide there in mist). Having enjoyed the views,
return to your car by the same route.

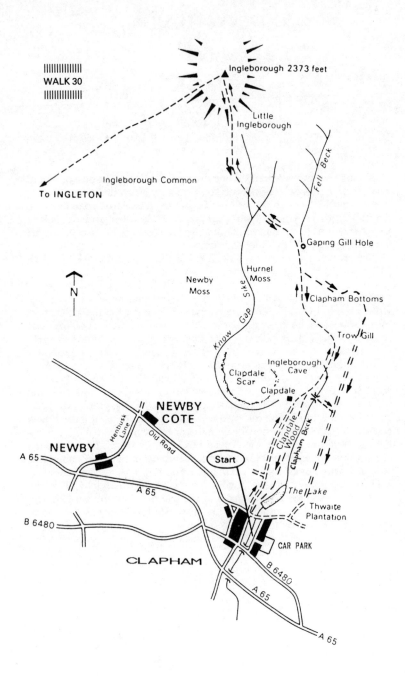

||||||||||||
WALK 30
||||||||||||

Ingleborough 2373 feet

Little
Ingleborough

Fell Beck

To INGLETON

Ingleborough Common

Gaping Gill Hole

N

Newby
Moss

Hurnel
Moss

Clapham Bottoms

Know Gap Sike

Trow Gill

Clapdale
Scar

Ingleborough
Cave

Clapdale

NEWBY
COTE

Henbusk Lane

Old Road

NEWBY

A 65

Start

Clapdale Wood

Clapham Beck

A 65

The Lake

B 6480

Thwaite
Plantation

CLAPHAM

CAR PARK

B 6480

A 65

A 65

INGLEBOROUGH

★

8 miles (13 km)

1:50 000 Sheet 98; 1:25 000 Outdoor Leisure Map 2 Yorkshire Dales
Western Area

This moderately strenuous ascent to a superb viewpoint passes one of
Yorkshire's show caves and its most spectacular pot-hole. Route-finding
is easy, but parts of the path can be wet. Note: An alternative return
route is given on a track which is not a right of way and on which walkers
have occasionally been stopped — the decision whether or not to use it is
yours.
   Park in the National Park carpark in Clapham (GR 745 693) (charge).
The Information Centre is worth a visit, and Clapham village is worth
exploring.

Turn right up the road for a few yards, then left over the footbridge,
then right again. At the top of the village bear left with the road, but
soon turn into a walled lane on the right signposted to Ingleborough,
Gaping Gill, Ingleborough Cave.
   Follow this track, ignoring subsidiary tracks forking left, all the way to
Clapdale Farm, and through the farmyard to a gate to the left of a barn.
Through this turn sharp right (signpost) downhill on a clear path. At the
bottom bear left along the track, with Clapham Beck to your right. Soon
you reach the entrance to Ingleborough Cave (one of Yorkshire's most
famous) which is open to visitors (charge).
   Continue along the track, crossing the bridge over the beck, which
emerges from under a cliff on the left. Some way on the track bears left,
and you cross a ladder-stile and begin the ascent of Trow Gill, gentle at
first, but with a short steep pull where the gorge closes in. Follow the
clear path, ignoring a ladder-stile in the wall on the left, until shortly
after you pass through another mini-limestone gorge the path leads you
to a double ladder-stile in this wall.
   Your path up the slope of Little Ingleborough in the distance is very
clear, as is the path under your feet. It leads to the fenced Gaping Gill,
one of England's most spectacular pot-holes, with Fell Beck flowing into
it. Take great care, and don't go near the edge.
   Your onward path bears left in front of the fence, now onto wetter
ground. It is badly eroded up Little Ingleborough. From the cairn at the
top of this steep pull there is a level stretch, with the main summit
straight ahead. The path slants up by the right, before bearing left over
the summit plateau.

After enjoying the extensive views, especially to the Lake District, but also to the Howgill Fells, Whernside and Penyghent, and exploring the summit, return by your outward route.

As the gradient eases on your descent from Little Ingleborough, you may be able to spot a grassy path forking right: this is in fact the true line of the right of way, much less badly eroded than the path you came up on, which passes well to the right of Gaping Gill. If you don't spot it, don't worry, because the two paths meet up again further on.

There is a pleasant **alternative descent** which does, however, involve using a track over which there is no right of way. To follow this alternative route return as far as the double ladder-stile then turn to [*] below.

Following the main route: Having passed Ingleborough Cave and reached the path climbing right to Clapdale, you have the choice of two alternative returns to Clapham: either straight ahead through the lovely grounds of the Ingleborough Hall Estate (small charge), or left over the footbridge, then up by the wall on your left to join a walled lane, in which you turn right, then right again at the T-junction some way later, to descend through two tunnels to Clapham near the church. When you reach the road turn left for the carpark.

[*] **Alternative descent:** (This does involve using a track over which there is no right of way.) After crossing the double ladder-stile, do not turn sharp right by the wall, but bear slightly right on a broad grassy path, obviously well-used. When you reach a limestone outcrop on the right there is a faint fork: keep left on the main path along the line of the limestone outcrop. At another, quite high limestone outcrop on the right, again make sure you keep left (i.e. straight ahead, not right towards a wood), down towards the valley of Clapham Bottoms. Twenty yards before you reach what look like the foundations of a limestone wall across your path, where the main path goes straight on, bear half-right on a narrower path, crossing the line of limestone near its right-hand end, and you will soon pick up a very good track descending into the valley bottom; this is well to the right of a low limestone escarpment.

Bear right with the track, but leave it where it bears left again and crosses the valley bottom: here keep straight head across the dip to join a track slanting up the other side towards a wall ahead, crossing another track in the valley bottom itself. Keep forward, slanting gently uphill, to pass through the left-hand of two gates facing you. In a few yards you pass through another gate, into the remains of an old walled lane. You are now back on a right of way. Follow this track/walled lane all the way back to Clapham, turning right at the T-junction to descend through two tunnels to the village near the church. When you reach the road turn left for the carpark.